THE BOOK MARKETING AUDIT

GET BETTER RESULTS BY HAVING A BETTER PLAN

KILBY BLADES

Dear Karen,
I hope this adds value
to your awesome marketing
track record!
all the Best,
Kilby

The Book Marketing Audit

Copyright © 2019 by Kilby Blades

Published by Luxe Press 2019

For permission requests and other inquiries, the publisher can be reached at: info@luxepress.net

KDP ISBN: 978-1-09-533823-0

For the marketers who share their failures so that others may succeed

CONTENTS

Introduction   vii

PART 1
THE PARTS WE MISS

1. Get Out of Jail Free   3
2. One Size Doesn't Fit All   21
3. Coffee is for Closers   29

PART 2
CLEAN YOUR OWN HOUSE

4. Order of Operations   35
5. Book Covers   39
6. Titles and Subtitles   45
7. Reviews   49
8. Blurbs   55
9. Pricing   63
10. Connecting the Dots   69
11. Add it Up   73

PART 3
GET IT DONE

12. Get it Done   85
13. DIY   87
14. Call in the Cavalry   91
15. You Can Do This   97
    Words of Thanks   99
    About Kilby Blades   101
    Also by Kilby Blades   103

INTRODUCTION

Why an Audit?

I know, I know. "Audit" is a sickening, awful, dirty word, and where do I get off using it in the title of a book about marketing? Audits are for taxes. For corporate compliance offices. For fraud investigations and insurance claims. If you had your 'druthers, you wouldn't be auditing anything—you'd be marketing harder and hoping to sell more books.

I'm here to tell you that there's no glory in marketing harder, and—as I think we can all agree—marketing harder is absolutely no fun. You've got books to write. Wine to drink. A rich, fulfilling life to lead. Marketing harder is the road to insanity and, too often, to financial ruin.

Auditing, on the other hand, examines the "why" of what you're doing. It exposes costly flaws and dangerous risks. It cares less about helping you fly faster down the track you're already on and more about making sure you're even on the right track.

The value of auditing is critically important, especially to authors, and especially now. During my 15-year career as a digital agency marketer, I spent more than $40 million of my clients' money. In all that time, I never saw another industry with such complex competition and such razor thin margins as publishing. No client group I've ever worked with has been so disadvantaged—nor so misled—as authors.

Most book marketing advice is imitation-based. It's designed to convince you that what worked for some other author is broadly effective and can therefore work for you. It doesn't take into account how good of a proxy you may be to the authors used to develop the methodology. The habit of auditing is what separates amateur marketers from professionals. Auditing is about trading commands for what to think for consciousness around *how* to think. It's about making smart decisions that are right for you and your individual brand.

This book will step you through conducting your own marketing self-audit. It is appropriate for authors at the published and pre-published stages. It will give indie authors specific guidance around how to research and execute improvements. It will give traditionally-published authors ammunition to negotiate, and a better understanding of what battles to pick with their publishers.

No matter what your publishing circumstances, it will improve your decision-making, place you in control, and salvage your most precious commodity: your time. Its overall goal is to leave you with confidence, empowerment, and complete understanding of your unique and very best marketing plan.

How This Book is Organized

Most of my marketing books are modular and friendly to skipping around. Not this one. I recommend that you read this one straight through. It's not long. It's not dense. But it carries a thread of logic that is linear in nature. And at various points, I build off of concepts raised in earlier parts of the book. Here's what I'll cover:

Part I. The Parts We Miss

Most brands are so eager to get their feet wet—if not swan dive—right into marketing that they forget to read the signs posted around the pool. Part I visits the foundational elements that people underestimate or miss. Chapter 1, "Get Out of Jail Free", is designed to orient you to your true goal, force you to get clear on your limits and constraints, and recalibrate your expectations accordingly. Chapter 2, "One Size Doesn't Fit All", talks about differentiated author libraries and the necessity of library-aligned marketing plans. Chapter 3, "Coffee is for Closers" introduces the final foundational concept: that there is no such thing as an isolated marketing tactic. Marketing always involves a complex, interrelated system of factors that contribute to the reader's decision to buy.

Part II. Clean Your Own House

With your mindset shifted toward thinking about your marketing uniquely and programmatically, it's time to gaze upon your own library with a critical eye. Part II helps you think through your brand's strengths and weaknesses, particularly as it pertains to your retail pages. One chapter each is dedicated to book covers, titles and subtitles, reader and editorial reviews, blurbs and pricing. The second-to-last chapter, "Connecting the Dots", talks about creating continuity through the use of back matter, fan ownership and tracking infrastructure. A final chapter, "Add it Up", helps you translate everything you've discovered about your brand strengths and weaknesses, and your library, into a specific, actionable and holistic marketing plan.

Part III. Get it Done

With your validated marketing strategy in-hand, it's time for execution. This means setting up and running new things that are important to your plan. This may also mean unwinding things that you don't need anymore or that violate one of your limits. Chapter 13, "DIY" offers tips and hacks for common marketing plan elements you may be executing yourself. Chapter 14, "Call in the Cavalry", discusses how to hire talent for anything you want to outsource. Finally, Chapter 15, "You Can Do This", are final words of wisdom and (you guessed it) a pep talk.

PART 1
THE PARTS WE MISS

1 GET OUT OF JAIL FREE

MARKETING FEELS LIKE AN ALBATROSS, doesn't it? Always heavy around your neck, the sharp tip of its curved beak impossible to ignore as it digs into your skin. For most authors, it's a burden. Even marketing geeks like me—people who actually *like* this stuff—struggle to find the time to write, as well as market, our own books.

As a marketing veteran who has worked with dozens of clients, I've met many an albatross over the years. They all tell the same story: an inability to be shrugged off of tired shoulders because their humans won't decide. Their humans haven't done enough real thinking about their own limits and what their marketing must do.

This first, critical chapter is about relieving you of your avian burden. You may never come to love marketing, but it doesn't have to suck. Here is what I can guarantee you: your burden will lighten by 80% once you've gained clarity and peace around the following three things: your real goal, your real limits, and forgiving yourself for what you can't do.

That's right—I used the word forgiveness. A lot of the stress we experience when it comes to marketing is about comparing ourselves to other authors and feeling we don't measure up. It's easy to taste sour grapes when we see authors whose writing is *just okay* hit bestseller lists and achieve wild commercial success. What's not so easy is looking hard at how that author got where she is, and being honest with ourselves about whether that thing she did lines up with what we're willing to do.

I hear this all the time from authors who come to me for advice, each with a sense that more readers await them and that they could be doing better. One hybrid author who had seen her $6,000 a month royalty income dwindle to $4,500 a month told me she wanted to take better control of the marketing for her indie titles and earn closer to $10,000. She was cycling through the same small set of Amazon ads that weren't working as well as they used to; her publisher was doing less than it ever had for her traditional releases; she'd been resting on her laurels and needed a reboot.

Her goal of $10,000 a month was within her reach—she'd been writing for a decade, had a recognizable name, solid reviews and she wrote in a big enough genre. She was barely using her mailing list, was not-at-all using Facebook, and was passing up fan engagement opportunities left and right. Yet when confronted with a solid plan for how to earn her $10,000 a month (and probably more), she scoffed at the time and investment that would be required.

Nothing that I suggested was outlandish: a strong, automated e-mail sequence, free books to serve as list bait and funnel people into her series...since this author felt that she had hit a plateau with Amazon ads, I suggested that she pay a good marketer to start her on Facebook. But she vetoed every suggestion.

This is where things get tricky. Because, whether we're aware of them or not, all of us have idiosyncrasies when it comes to our attitudes about craft and the business of our writing. This author didn't believe in freebies under any circumstances and couldn't get over the price tag for the fair wage of a skilled marketer. Mind you, the plan was solid—a tried-and-true approach for authors with libraries like hers—and she would have made back her money. Her problem wasn't that her goal was unachievable—it was that what she thought she wanted didn't align to what she was prepared to do.

This is where most of us misstep: we want the results but we either don't know or haven't come to terms with exactly what it would take to achieve them. Because most of us are vague on the details, or in denial about the tradeoffs involved, we're left to watch those who have figured it out excel. Watching other people attain goals that seem constantly to evade us only underscores our suspicion that we're failing.

The antidote is to simply get real—about what you truly want to achieve, about what personal time and elbow grease you're willing to expend, and your advantages and disadvantages as an author. The burden lifts (and the exciting, fulfilling part begins) when you spit out your sour grapes and begin to live in self-forgiveness and truth.

YOUR REAL GOAL

Something I ask my audience when I teach The Book Marketing Audit live is: what do you need your marketing to achieve? The initial response is always some combination of awkward silence and "are you kidding?"-type stares. Walking into the course, students honestly believe that they are all there for a single, common, reason. By the time some brave soul speaks up and says he's there to sell more books, the whole class is looking at me like I'm crazy, because, *duh*.

The first thing you must know about book marketing is that your real goal *isn't* to sell more books. Your real goal is more personal than that. Moving more product will get you *closer* to that thing you want—something tied to your individual circumstances and maybe your ego needs—but there's no such thing as selling books just for the sake of it. Maybe authoring isn't your day job, but you really want it to be, and, in your day job, you earn a $50,000 salary. Your goal isn't just to sell more books—it's to sustainably earn an extra $50,000 per year in royalties.

The mistake most authors make is being vague about what they want, or adopting a settling mindset—telling themselves they'd be happy with some squishier outcome. It's not enough to wax poetic about making your new series kick butt or rejuvenating your backlist performance. If $50,000 more a year is what you need, own it.

This may seem like an audacious—maybe even unthinkable—goal if you're not even close to earning money like this. But if making quit-your-job money is your endgame, you have to start thinking in those terms. I'm sure you've heard the saying, "a goal without a plan is just a wish". This concept is gospel when it comes to marketing. There is no way to know what mix of tactics you should try, how intensely you should pursue them, and how much money you should be spending if you're not crystal clear on what it is you're trying to do.

That brings me to the second thing you must know about book marketing (and any marketing, really): different goals prescribe different marketing approaches. The approach you would take to earning a steady, predictable writing income is different from the one you would take to hit a bestseller list. Many people believe that highly successful authors have all found the same holy grail of marketing wisdom and are working the same secret plan, only at different scales. Nothing could be farther from the truth. Authors do well who are working toward their own goals in the smartest possible ways based on how their own libraries are constructed. Can't figure out yours? Let's look at some common author goals:

- **To break even.** There's no shame in a pragmatic goal like not losing money on your authoring. Plenty of people who choose to write don't rely on the income. Even those who don't need to *make* money from authoring may not want to *lose* money, and the lifestyle costs of being a writer add up. Going to writing retreats, conferences, doing workshops and taking classes can amount to thousands of dollars each year.

- **To earn $x per year.** Many authors do need the income to keep food on the table. Even among those who don't, there may be a vanity amount they'd like to make. That sort of mindset goes back to personal beliefs about money. Some authors are looking to hit a certain income level to convince themselves (or, more often, a spouse) that authoring isn't a hobby, it's a career. The trick with this goal is to be real about how much money you want or need to make. If you don't acknowledge the real number, you can't possibly build the right plan.

- **To bask in glory and accolades.** Some people are in it for the fame, and if not Nora Roberts or Stephen King fame, for bragging rights at least. Hitting a big bestseller list like the New York Times, USA Today, or Wall Street Journal is the dream (read: obsession) of many an author. Lists like those work in a highly-specific way. If making it onto one of them is your goal, your marketing plan must be different than it would be for any other objective: long-term crescendo-building and release planning that is executed with precision timing are needed to meet this goal.

- **To cultivate a dedicated, evangelist fan base.** If you're like me, you care more about appreciation for your creative work than you care about anything else. I'd rather sell 5,000 books a year to readers who will treasure my every word and come to a signing if I'm in their city than to sell 5,000,000 books a year to fickle binge-readers who will buy my book today but forget my name next month.

- **To build your brand toward some secondary purpose.** Sometimes, there's a bigger picture—one in which your marketing incentives are tied to a separate goal. If your true passion is to coach other authors or teach industry-focused classes, showing that your own books have done well (via sales, reviews, awards, rankings, lists, etc.) lends necessary credibility. There are other cases in which authors want to show well for others. If you're in the market for a new agent and you're already published, prospective agents will snoop on your sales. And it's not just agents. A litany of industry folks are always looking at author sales and rankings for editorial and other opportunities.

This isn't a cafeteria and the above is not a menu. In other words, you don't have to pick from the list. But you do have to think deeply and authentically about what you really want. This may require a long walk in the woods, a hot bath and a glass of wine, or a conscious deprogramming of the not-so-useful messages you've been hearing about book marketing for years: that you're never doing enough and that the only goal is more.

The only goal is *not* more. Your goal is yours alone. And I want you to stop and think deeply about what that really is. I mean it. Stop. Think it through, and write it down.

YOUR REAL LIMITS

I'll never forget the month-long back-and-forth I went through with my mother while planning my wedding. She and my dad had offered to pay for the affair. They weren't rich, but I'm their daughter, and they'd likely spent a decade dreaming about giving me a nice wedding. They'd squirreled money away in true doting-parent style. I kept asking my mother what the budget was—how much she and my dad were looking to contribute. My now-husband and I wanted to know their number so that we could budget what we'd spend on the rest.

My mom kept saying, "'Don't worry about the money. Have the wedding you want." At some point, I called her bluff, citing a number I knew was wildly out of her league. "Fine," I told her. "We want to spend a hundred-thousand dollars." You know what happened next: after a very hearty laugh, she was forced to say out loud what the real budget was.

Everybody has limits, though many of us are taught to avoid admitting them, certainly to other people and often to ourselves. Too many of us agree to take on more than we can handle, not because we actually *can* do it all—because those around us seem to be doing it all, and we wish we also could. Figuring out your own limits is about reconciling the kinds of outcomes you're hoping to see with the real (not imagined) effort required to drive those results.

Even someone who only writes how-to comic books about underwater basket weaving can be successful in this business. If he hires a good enough cover designer, a PR firm that cooks up a good enough angle and a marketer who runs world-class campaigns, he's got a shot at Good Morning America and a best-seller list. The point is, most things can be achieved with enough resources, whether that be money or expertise. But you only have so many dollars in the bank and so many hours in a day. You can't get to the right marketing plan without understanding the limits of your own resources—and one of those resources is you.

So, answer the following questions about your time resources. The answers shouldn't be overly-optimistic, like your new year's resolution to lose twenty pounds. Answer these questions, not like you would on January 2nd, but on February 1st —with a harsh sense of reality and your many competing priorities in mind:

- How many hours per week are you truly willing to spend on marketing?
- Are you proficient enough in any tasks you would like to do on your own to work quickly and efficiently? Conversely, are there certain areas where you have no natural talent and will never be able to do something well yourself? (e.g., graphic design, blurb writing, ad campaign optimization)
- Are you willing to be responsive on social media or adopt marketing habits that may interrupt your writing flow?
- Are you willing to spend time to develop more original content (for newsletters, freebie content and other purposes) that are not book manuscripts?

Next, ask yourself the following questions about financial resources:

- How much can you comfortably afford to spend on marketing each month?

- Are you willing to lose money at the beginning if you think it serves a long-term goal? By when would you want to see profits?
- Is there a specific Return on Investment (ROI) that you expect for your effort? (e.g., do you believe that earning $1.05 for every dollar spent on marketing may not be worth your effort but that $2.50 for every dollar spent, is?)
- If you aren't willing or able to perform certain tasks yourself, are you willing to pay fair market value to have a skilled professional do it in your stead?

You'll notice I used the term "skilled professional" and "fair market value". This is deliberate language. In marketing, quality really matters. Chances are, the authors whose brands you admire are not halfway-doing anything—they're working with (or have themselves worked hard to become) much-better-than-average cover designers and blurb writers, and are running much-better-than-average marketing campaigns.

Finally, ask yourself the following questions about emotional resources:

- Are you willing to repeatedly fail before you succeed and to make expensive mistakes?
- Are you willing to entrust helpers who you hire with your brand and your sensitive information?
- Are you willing to take on being the boss and managing others to help you with your marketing?
- Are you willing to endure the learning curve required to gain professional-level proficiency in any area that you won't hire a professional for?

I know, I know—these are all tough questions. Intimidating,

even. You probably feel like you're in some twisted, publishing-world version of *Scared Straight*. I'm not exactly trying to scare you. I'm trying to orient you, very quickly, to your own very best marketing plan—a plan that satisfies your true goal, and one that your bank account, personal limits, emotional health and competing priorities can survive.

Thinking about limits always makes me think about a specific author-friend who taught me an important lesson. Unlike me, she's not a marketer, but she's serious about being hugely profitable at selling books. She is a mom of three—young twins and a singleton—attends lovingly to parenting and manages her household, and is wickedly smart with an advanced science degree.

We began self-publishing around the same time and had many healthy debates about how to use advertising to build our readership. I argued that you have to spend money to make money and was willing to put thousands of dollars at risk if it meant getting to my brand's success formula faster. She, on the other hand, did not want to lose even a single dollar and was willing to only start small—to build slowly and carefully, and to never spend more on marketing than she was bringing in.

I'll admit, I thought she was nuts—that her plan would never succeed and that it would take her months to gain insights and results that a more aggressive campaign could have gotten her in days or weeks. I wasn't even sure she would learn anything with a budget too small to bring in a steady stream of traffic. She was the tortoise and I was the hare, and as I looked around at what other authors were doing, I mostly saw hares winning. Whereas she was slow and steady, I was fast, eager to make things happen, and confident that it would all pay off.

So, whose plan was best? The answer is both. Each of us achieved our goals and did so with minimal angst by knowing, and staying true to, our limits. She respected her own financial boundaries by never being more than $200 in debt from advertising at any given moment. She had the patience to crowdsource her learning and the stamina to stick with slow-moving campaigns. She also knew that she never wanted marketing to take such a front seat that it would displace her time for writing. Because she'd thought it through and understood her own habits and tendencies, her priorities were clear and her expectations were realistic.

I also achieved my goal to learn as much as possible as quickly as possible. I was comfortable treating my early marketing budget as a sunk cost. I didn't lose sleep over any huge failure (even though there were a few) and willingness to take risks compelled me to try some out-of-the-box approaches that worked well. Conservatism didn't fit for what I was trying to achieve, and I thrived emotionally from the sense of progress and experimentation. I knew exactly how to test and what to try.

My wish for you is that you make the same peace with your own marketing plan—that you're so clear on what you're trying to do and how you're going to go about it, that it's not a source of constant re-evaluation and stress.

So, go back and reread those questions—every single one. Think hardest about the ones you're tempted to avoid. Write your answers down. Don't worry—this is the last time I'll ask you to stop and do something that feels tedious. But this is important. It's time to change the conversation you're having with yourself about what you are or aren't achieving, and why.

DOING **the Math on Your Goals**

Let's take a look at the four things I asked you to think through:

- Your goal, which must be specific and measurable
- Your time constraints

- Your financial constraints
- Your emotional constraints

With all four of these elements laid out, side by side, for you to face unflinchingly, does feasibility suddenly look different? Let's say your list looks something like this. Can it realistically work?

- **Goal:** To hit the USA Today Bestseller List this year
- **Time constraints:** 3 hours per week on marketing
- **Financial constraints:** $250 per month to spend on marketing
- **Emotional constraints:** Given lack of proficiency in marketing, wants to hire an expert to help

Even without knowing anything about this author's library—the strength of his fan base or his ability to drive organic sales from his mailing list or calling in favors, I'm fairly certain he can't achieve his goal given these constraints.

Even authors who are already topping the charts with much-anticipated releases are still spending big advertising dollars and pulling out all the stops to support healthy launches. Even if they're not invested in making a list, they are invested in the hugely positive halo effect from the visibility that comes with sustained rankings.

Now, imagine that I knew more about this author's library: that he publishes only twice a year, all in a tightly-connected series with a low sell-through rate. Suppose he has a 5,000-person newsletter and is getting, at most, 100 pre-orders on each new title. Based on this author's individual circumstances and constraints, he needs much more time and money—not to mention stamina to endure working ten times as hard on marketing—in order to reach his goal.

I know this may seem like an exaggerated example. Believe me when I tell you that I see a lot of authors who are far from what they want and living in denial about just how far. I'm not here to crush your hopes and dreams or to sound defeatist if these resemble your circumstances and goals. But I do want you to start living in truth: your chances of hitting the USA Today Bestseller List this year, if these are your constraints and if this is the state of your brand's health, are slim to none.

Only when you see your own picture clearly can the real planning begin. If this were really you, you couldn't achieve USA Today bestseller status in the near-term because you neither have a ready-and-waiting earned follower base to kick off your sales nor do you have the budget to advertise your way into selling the balance of books you would need to, to make that list. There's other evidence that advertising may not be cost-efficient, as the current series hasn't earned many evangelists given weak sell-through rates, which probably means the retail pages aren't full of gushing five-star reviews about your other work.

If you hold this goal as constant, the path forward is clear: to earn a solid base of super-fans and groom them well so that you have mailing list support to make your next launch huge. Getting real may also spark creativity. Realizing that you're far off financially to support large-scale campaigning could compel you to find a way to raise the money. Conversely, the very act of understanding just how many of your own limits it would violate to achieve your goal may cause you to decide that the goal isn't as important to you as you thought.

HOW CLOSE (or Far) Are You?

The rule of thumb is this: the "bigger" your goal, the fewer real constraints there must be, not only on your time and money but on how quickly you're willing to write and release. Entire books have been written on release strategy and timing. Many authors who are doing well are publishing more than half-a-million words per year. This underscores why what is achievable for you has to be seen through the spectacle of your willingness to do whatever it takes vs. making peace with your limits.

All of this is complicated by the fact that, beyond your personal goals and constraints, your own library will have its own strengths and weaknesses. To look back at the common author goals I listed earlier, here are broad generalizations around what is typically required to achieve each from a time, financial, and emotional commitment perspective alone:

- **Breaking even.** If your goal is to break even, it's all about doing the math. Figure out the incremental amount you need to earn (beyond your current baseline) and use royalties-per-book to calculate what that translates into, in terms of copies sold. If you need to sell an extra 200 books a month and you're underutilizing your current resources (like your mailing list, back matter and other free-ish and easy-ish opportunities), you're in a good position to do it on the cheap. But if you need to sell an extra 1,500 books a month and/or you're already squeezing your current program to perform as well as it can, your plan will only work if you're not overly constrained by budget and your ability to learn or hire talent to manage your ads.
- **Reaching a specific dollar amount.** Similar to breaking even, you have to do the math. How many books do you need to sell, net of the cost of

advertising and other expenses, to get to your number? Do your upcoming releases have a natural advantage, such as a predecessor to feed into it or do you need to sell the book as its own brand new first-in-universe title or standalone? The larger your target profit amount, the stronger the likelihood that there will be an advertising component. This means that you'll need out-of-pocket advertising dollars and the time to manage the campaigns yourself or to hire someone to do it. You'll also need a plan for managing your fan community in order to support future releases. From the time and expense involved in all of this, you must also offset the fees you will pay your advertiser to reach net profitability.

- **Bestseller status.** Bestseller status is typically achieved by showing outstanding sales over a series of days, with every list-issuing body tracking to its own evaluation period and rules. The USA Today list counts sales from Monday to Sunday, only counts sales in the United States, and has other requirements around what price point and distribution guidelines must be met in order to be considered. If you don't have huge print distribution or are not traditionally published, USA Today is the most attainable bestseller list. The Publisher's Weekly and Wall Street Journal lists work off of Nielsen Book Scan data, which cares more about traditional print retailer sales. The New York Times tracks from Monday to Monday and admits that it bases its list at least partially off of print sales. It has been called everything from arbitrary to secretive. Educating yourself around how each list you want to hit actually works is a must if this is your goal. Many authors believe that you simply have to get into a top-tier sales volume range, regardless of where, when and how you're selling, but this simply isn't true.

- **To bask in other accolades.** If you simply want recognition for the quality of your work, or big, shiny award seals to stick on your covers, get into the habit of entering literary contests and awards. They often cost money to enter, but some of them come with cash prizes. Winning awards carries no pressure to sell actual books.

- **To cultivate a dedicated fan base.** If this is your real goal, shifting your money (and your attentions) to social media, newsletter execution and attending fan events is what's required. Beyond strengthening relations with your existing fan base, your plan will need a sustainable, affordable way for you to gradually funnel in new fans. This tactic mainly requires time and the ability to split your attention in order to socially engage. If your time and effort constraints don't gel with this goal, you may have to make a shift.

- **Brand-building.** If you're looking to build a brand that shows very well, focus on accolades and social proof. Get reviews, both editorial and reader-based in nature. Win awards. Make guest appearances on blogs and podcasts and at events. Show off how impressive you are.

FORGIVING YOURSELF. **For Real.**

By now you see where I'm going with the forgiveness thing.

Forgiving yourself frees your albatross. So many authors beat themselves up over not being able to achieve marketing and sales goals they never stop to realize they don't really want or can't possibly swing based on their current, individual circumstances. There is nothing shameful about not being able to find an extra ten hours a week to spend on marketing, let alone an extra $1,000 a month to help get you to the next tier. We have children to raise. Adult parents to care for. Pets to love. Bills to pay. Sometimes the math doesn't add up.

All that some of us need is this reality check—this acknowledgement that we're not actually failing. And for someone to say out loud that despite the many, many authors who want you to believe they're doing just fine, marketing is killing them, too. There's value in admitting that this business is harder than ever—that publishers expect authors to bear the burden of marketing and that our paltry royalties, whether we're traditional or indie, are so-very-razor-thin.

So let lie what you can't or don't want to do. Rethink goals, limits, or both, if necessary. And get ready to think through your marketing plan as a factor of the next big variable: your library.

2 ONE SIZE DOESN'T FIT ALL

I ALWAYS CRINGE when I see book marketing courses that dangle the carrot of wild success, propping up examples of satisfied authors who have used the methodology and made gobs of money. I've bought some of these courses. Many are quite pricey and—to be fair—many of them are quite good. The problem is, they're rarely transparent about their own fine print.

The plain truth is that not every marketing approach can work for every author. A plan that's bulletproof and game-changing for Author A may be the absolute-wrong plan for Author B. Most book marketing courses are so bent on hard-selling the instructor's expertise that they don't stop to mention the specific characteristics an author needs in order to be successful. I'm not saying you *shouldn't* take book marketing courses—you'll need a fitting one of you decide to do your own management rather than hiring a pro. What I am saying is that one size doesn't fit all, and that marketing for your specific library composition matters.

.   .   .

FOUR VERY DIFFERENT AUTHORS

Let's consider the hypothetical profiles of four very different authors:

- **Author A** is a traditionally-published New York Times Bestseller with more than fifteen book releases to her name and upwards of a hundred high-average reviews for every book. She only writes series, and all of her series include at least 3 volumes; her most popular series is currently on book 7. She writes full time and turns out 3 to 4 books per year in a niche genre with long-term, dedicated readers.

- **Author B** is an indie author who published his debut novel less than six months ago and is live with only two releases. He's not sure when he'll publish his next book and, overall, doesn't have a rhythm, plan or schedule around how many books per year he plans to release. He writes in a large, saturated genre with tens of thousands of titles in competition with his and his current releases are light on reviews.

- **Author C** is a hybrid author who writes across several genres. The covers of the books she self-published look different from the covers developed by the traditional house she's contracted with. The fact that she writes in different genres dilutes her brand consistency even more. Despite these anomalies, her individual books show well and have a lot of positive reviews.

- **Author D** is a 20-year authoring veteran with an enormous, but lackluster, library. Some of her covers are very old and look dated. Over time, there have been changes to the kinds of tropes she writes, but

she's always played in the same genre. She writes
mostly standalones and is on the brink of reversion
for some of her books' rights.

Now, imagine that these four authors are all taking the same
marketing course—receiving identical advice about how to
improve their sales. Whatever the course is teaching—I don't care
how "good" the course is reputed to be—there is zero chance that
the advice is equally relevant to all four. Following advice that
can't possibly work for their own libraries is a top reason why
authors fail at marketing. They take the wrong course, read the
wrong book, follow advice that's wrong for them. Many hours of
effort and often many marketing dollars later, they're not getting
the sales they want and they're banging their heads against a wall.

The reasons for this are easy to understand once you dig into
the assumptions. Mark Dawson's *Ads for Authors* course is excel-
lent and the information contained within it is spot-on. Yet, if you
take the course you'll quickly see that Dawson's approach comes
with certain expectations. It assumes that you're willing to use
freebies as list bait, that you're willing to go heavy on your
mailing list, and that your library is set up for each book to hook
the next. The Mark Dawson course would be great for Author A
and Author D.

Author B is in a different position. With only two titles
released, he can't do much with freebies unless he either makes
one of his two books free or writes a few brand-new, short-form
freebies specifically for his mailing list. Doing the former would
cut his royalties in half at the same time he's spending more time
and marketing dollars to hook new readers. Cranking out mailing
list freebies will take away precious time he needs to focus on his
more important goal: to finish his next full-length, full-priced
novel that will improve his bottom line.

Author C would also be hard-pressed to go big on a strategy

that focuses on sell-through. Readers who love her Suspense/Thrillers may want nothing to do with her Romance and it's possible that working with a single multi-genre newsletter would do more harm than good. She might do better with a niche marketing course containing tips and tricks for authors who write under the same name in numerous genres.

An auditing mentality is useful here. Before you spend a single dollar or a single minute on a new marketing approach, think critically about how a specific approach gels with your library. I almost have a coronary any time I see book marketing advice insisting that "every author" should be doing this or that. Each author has different tools in their toolkit, different advantages and disadvantages—different things going for them.

THE LIBRARY-LEVEL AUDIT

In Part II, we'll be talking about retail pages—how to look at your own strengths and weaknesses, title by title, retailer by retailer, and page by page. But first, let's tackle the bigger economics. The size and structure of your library as a whole is the most important driver of your ability to passively and inexpensively sell books. The key concept here is sell-through and the basic logic is simple: when one book naturally leads to another, it takes less time, money and effort to sell more books.

SERIES AND UNIVERSES

The easiest way to create sell-through is via the use of series and universes. Cliffhangers compel readers to keep buying to see how a story—or a saga—ends. If readers in your genre hate cliffies, standalones in a common-universe series are hugely popular. In genres like Women's Fiction, series aren't common, but it's still possible to sell through your library if your writing has a common thread. All that sell-through potential really requires is similarity that your reader will latch on to: maybe it's a trope, maybe it's a theme, maybe it's a particular kind of setting that shows itself in numerous books.

This logic carries to non-fiction books as well. Patrick Lencioni's series are a shining example. His leadership fables discuss corporate culture, teams and organizational health. No two books are about the exact same thing, but they're geared toward the same target reader—titles like *Death by Meeting, Silos, Politics & Turf Wars*, and *The Five Dysfunctions of a Team* are distinct, but related.

If your library has this sort of potential, a common strategy is to spend marketing dollars on only the first book and trusting readers to follow the daisy-chain. It's not a tragedy to sell the first book at a loss or to go perma-free with the first in a series if you make up the money on subsequent books. In order to understand the economics of this strategy, do analysis on your own track record.

This is easiest if your books are sequential. Do 50% of those who buy the first book buy the second? What percentage of readers buy the third? The fourth? The fifth? Factor in royalties for each book and do the algebra. You should be able to get to a dollar amount for each series you're looking at: an average result that tells how much you typically earn from each new person who picks up your first book.

The ability to sell through in this way is a major advantage in book marketing. Writing series and universes isn't for everyone, but there's a reason why so many marketing-minded authors have adopted the practice. A huge determinant of the marketing approach you use will be the strength and magnitude of your sell-through opportunity. Magnitude relates to the size of your library. Your sell-through potential will be different for a 20-book universe than it will be if you're writing trilogies. Your use of companion works, such as prequels and epilogues for fiction and workbooks or the like for non-fiction, will also boost your cross-selling and upselling ability.

BACKLISTS

Even if your books aren't really related, having a robust back-list can be a strength, especially if your library has been consistent over time. Many authors (the lucky ones) have fans who simply love their writing—fans who will read whatever they put out, no matter the genre. This is when having a backlist comes in handy—some percentage of new readers will reach the end of their gateway book or series, look at what else you've got, and keep plowing through. In Part II, I'll talk about auditing your back matter to get the most out of your backlist and conscious planning around how to step your readers through.

SHALLOW AND SINGLE-TITLE LIBRARIES

Not having many titles in your library places you at a natural disadvantage. Particularly in fiction, binge-reading is real. Any reader who loves what you write may want more of it, right now. But if you don't have something at the ready, they often move on. Think about it from their perspective: unless you have a pre-order page up for an upcoming title, or unless the back matter of your existing books clearly outlines your release plan, readers have no idea what's next or whether anything new is coming at all. If this is your situation, having a very strong mailing list is critical. The goal is to stay connected. In the absence of opportunities to feel connected to you through your characters, your advice or your wisdom, your newsletter serves as a necessary proxy.

Another thing: this may not be such a big deal if you're with a traditional publisher. Chances are, they're handling your marketing, you got an advance or made some minimum amount on your book. The better publishers organize sales-boosters like PR coverage, critical reviews, and they advertise your work to their own hard-earned mailing lists. They're taking a big percentage, but they're also covering the upfront costs. They know all about momentum and release schedules and they likely are in process already with you and your next book.

For indie authors, who spend money out-of-pocket on everything, the financial stakes to marketing an early library tend to be high. The economics are often abysmal—it may cost you $3.00 to earn a new reader on a book that only brings in $2.35 in royalties per copy sold. Add in what you paid for cover design, formatting software, ISBNs, editing and any other expenses you incurred and it takes a lot of sales to earn back what you put out.

The catch-22 is unfortunate. On one hand, you want readers. You've put your masterpiece out there, and you want to see it become relevant and enjoyed. You want people to leave reviews and you want for your book to do decently in the rankings to signal to new, prospective readers that your book doesn't suck. You're also thinking about your next book, which you know will be harder to sell if your first book appeared to be unsuccessful. For the sake of your brand, there are incentives to project the image of success. The deeply-unsatisfying truth about shallow, early libraries is that you may have to sink money upfront into building your author brand.

Admittedly, this pivots somewhat on what you write, and non-fiction fares a bit better. Even debut non-fiction authors can get away with charging $9.99 for an eBook if the topic is timely, interesting, or adds freshness to a space that no one else has written on in 5 or more years. Fiction is tougher. Both literature and genre fiction are saturated and competitive. Ad costs are high, and without a recognizable name or other signals that might validate your work, readers won't pay more than $3.99 or $4.99 for an eBook.

LIBRARIES OF NONE

If it wasn't clear before, let it be clear now that knowing all of this upfront is an advantage. The smartest authors I know researched marketing before they published a single word. Plenty of authors gunning for commercial success, or even just trying not to go into debt understand the advantages I describe and are writing entire series up front. The point is, if you're not published yet, take the time to do all of the smart things those of us who dove in blindly wished we'd had the knowledge to do.

- Consider writing a universe if you like the idea of selling through a series.
- Universe or not, consider rapid release (a few weeks apart) to keep binge-readers hooked.
- Consider releasing no more than three months apart so that you can have a link to pre-order your next book in the back matter of the previous one.
- Build a killer newsletter sequence if you won't release frequently and want to keep readers warm between books.
- Think through other elements of your brand that could keep you connected before you pursue your release.

3 COFFEE IS FOR CLOSERS

HAVE you ever seen the movie *Glengarry Glenross*? Yes, I know it's a Pulitzer Prize-winning play. David Mamet's Broadway production won Tony Awards for both the original and the revival. The film version is fantastically acted with a scene so iconic, it's been parodied on *Saturday Night Live*, with Alec Baldwin reprising his role as the memorable and menacing corporate overseer, Blake.

The story follows bedraggled salesmen struggling to make their quotas. Their job is to sell junk real estate to people who are basically poor. Somewhere along the line, these leads have agreed to be contacted about investment opportunities, but most don't want to buy. In the "coffee is for closers" scene, the salesmen complain that they're not making their quotas because they're being given cold leads. According to the salesmen, the problem isn't them, it's the prospective buyers. Beneath Blake's brusqueness and toxic masculinity, hidden truisms about sales arise. It's not enough to stand in front of a prospect, hand outstretched and hoping with minimal persuasion that they'll buy—you have to know how to close the deal.

Too many authors underestimate this. They focus energies on driving traffic—on ad clicks and newsletter swaps and anything else that will expose new readers to their books. Most book marketing advice treats it as a foregone conclusion that your book has the ability to sell—that you'd be doing better if more readers and the right readers were exposed to you.

As any marketer will tell you, or any salesperson for that matter, that really isn't how sales and marketing work. It's not about getting better leads. It's about making the best case when you have your prospect in pocket. The famous "Always Be Closing" speech delivered by Alec Baldwin in *Glengarry Glenross* homes in on this: every second of your prospect's attention must be used to get you closer to the sale.

A big piece of the auditing approach is getting real about what plays out for your prospective reader during the precious seconds they spend on your retail page. I don't care if you're running the best ad campaign in the world and getting 10,000 retail page views a day. If your cover looks unprofessional, your blurb is a mess, and your reviews are bad, your awesome ad campaign doesn't matter. I don't want you to spend a single advertising dollar on a book that can't sell.

It is because of this issue that I was inspired to write *The Book Marketing Audit*. At the time, I was still doing hands-on work running marketing campaigns for clients. Conversations with my new clients would usually go something like this:

Client: I'd like to hire you to run my Facebook campaigns.

Me: Great. Show me which books you'd like to market.

Client: (shows me a retail page with a book that has five lukewarm reviews, a just-okay book cover, and a hard-to-follow blurb)

Me: I don't think Facebook will help you. Let's focus on your retail pages.

Client: What?! Why?

Me: Because this page can't convert.

It's usually at around that point that I navigate down to their category, open their sub-genre in a new window, and show them their book next to category bestsellers. "This," I tell them,"...is what is selling in your genre today."

I'll be honest—most authors are skeptical of the notion their retail pages aren't working. They may be in love with their book covers. Their blurb makes perfect sense to them. If they don't have many reviews, or if the reviews aren't great, they've surrendered to their own circumstances. Often, they've even rationalized a story around it. (e.g. "The people who left bad reviews are trolls" or "It's too hard to get reviews, so I've moved on and am focused on something I can control.")

Yet, retail pages are critical. Readers get there after expressing mild interest. They saw your book in search results, on a social share or maybe through an ad. The job of the retail page is to strengthen that interest. They were curious enough to click, but clicking on whatever got them to you doesn't mean they're ready to buy. Your retail page has to sway them from casual curiosity to real interest. And every element of your page has to perform.

This is one area in which indie authors may actually have an advantage. Publishers can be tone deaf or slow to the uptake when it comes to pivoting on what the market wants. Whereas publishers are queuing up releases a year or more in advance and worrying about imprint branding and alignment, indies are flexible to making changes and fine-tuning retail pages.

Indies also have an advantage when it comes to testing. By virtue of having control of your own page, you can run experiments on variations of your own assets to see what combinations work best. The sum of implementing best practices and testing to improve conversion rates makes for a solid optimization approach.

Traditionally-published authors are in a different situation. The quality of marketing teams inside publishing houses varies, as does the support a given author might receive. The bigger authors get the bigger marketing budgets, which does not bode well if you're a small fry. Some authors are fighting for their publishers to do something more—*anything* more—to help market their books for them.

Even when the level of effort a publisher puts in to help sell a book is strong, the publisher may not be inclined to include authors in many marketing decisions. Regardless of your situation as a traditionally-published author, there's leverage to be had if you can bring real insights to the table.

For example, if you hate the blurb your publisher wrote for you, and you think you've got something better, do an A/B test in your newsletter and see whether the one you prefer works. If it does, take that insight to your publisher. Be data-driven and give them numbers—the more impressive the delta, the better.

There are many, many reasons why your publisher probably won't make that kind of change, but showing your savvy marketing chops will pay off with some publishers. They're in this to make money, too. If you consistently bring them ideas, insights and observations that could bolster your sales while maintaining the integrity of their line, the better ones will come to view you as a trusted partner.

PART 2
CLEAN YOUR OWN HOUSE

4 ORDER OF OPERATIONS

DO you remember order of operations? That rule you learned in math class about how to solve equations? When I was a kid, the mnemonic was "Please Excuse My Dear Aunt Sally." It taught tiny mathematicians that, when faced with a problem involving numerous signs, to do the math in Parentheses first, then Exponents, then Multiplication, Division, Addition and Subtraction, in that order.

Readers who visit your retail pages are also doing math. They're considering a number of factors and coming to an answer as to whether your book is one they'd like to read. As with mathematical equations, there's also an order to what readers look at first. As you prioritize what elements of your own pages need work, keep this concept in mind.

ORDER OF OPERATIONS **in Book Buying**

I know, I know. Different readers care about different things. You could argue that people who trust the wisdom of crowds go straight to the reviews for social proof and that detail-oriented, data-driven people skip over everything else to get right to the blurb. This is true for some percentage of people. However, my hypothesis takes into account the way retail pages are laid out and what the retailers have conditioned users to focus on.

In the advertising industry, we call the most prominent parts of an online retail page the parts that appear "above the fold". This refers to the way that the front pages of printed newspapers have always been constructed. Since you can only see the top half of the page as it sits on the news stand (the part above the fold) whatever headlines and images appear there have to be strong enough to sell a lot of papers.

In the book selling business, I believe the ordered importance of assets is as follows:

1. **Book Covers.** In book search results, covers tend to be the most prominent element. On retail pages, covers tend to appear on the top left. In the largest markets, readers speak languages that read top to bottom, left to right. Add in the fact that covers are colorful and eye-catching and you can be sure: that's where reader attention is going first. Covers are even more important on secondary retailers like iTunes and Barnes and Noble; their pages are a lot less crowded than Amazon's. While Amazon is busy syndicating author blog postings, offering blurb previews, and hosting ads nearly everywhere, other retailers have "cleaner" pages that place greater emphasis on the cover alone.

2. **Price and Format.** Apart from covers, price and format are two more elements that every retailer goes out of its way to display prominently. Price boxes on Amazon are larger than the space that shows ballpark reviews. On retailers like Kobo and

iTunes, reviews are somewhat subordinated in terms of page placement. On nearly every retailer, price is not.

3. **Ballpark Rating and Number of Reviews.** Most product pages and some search engine results pages give a visual on star rating, usually in the same eye line as the cover. To actually read reviews, users may have to scroll down or click off to another page. But, in most cases, visitors get a ballpark sense for how well the book is rated, above the fold.

4. **Titles and Subtitles.** Similar to book covers, titles and subtitles are prominently displayed. They are low on the list because, believe it or not, readers skip over titles and subtitles. They might make it a point to look if they want to understand what number the volume may be in a series. Usually, reading this element is redundant. It's information that any well-designed cover has already told them.

5. **Blurbs.** Most users will have already felt some gut reaction to whether they're interested in your book by the time they make it to your blurb (that is, *if* they even make it to your blurb—more on that in a minute). Even then, people don't like reading large chunks of text. Some users skip over blurbs entirely because they want easier-to-digest information to help them to decide whether to buy your book.

6. **Editorial Reviews.** At the end of the day, all readers want is a sure thing. They want to know that, if they spend good money to buy a book, they'll learn something of value or be told a story they'll remember and treasure. Endorsement from someone with credibility is enough to sway certain readers to

buy your book. Editorial reviews are rarely above the fold. On some retailers, you have to scroll to get to them. On Barnes & Noble, you even have to click onto a separate tab.

7. **Detailed Review Content.** Individual reviews may also be very important to certain readers. As these are always below the fold, readers who care about them will have to dig. Another reason why these are subordinated on the list is because, if there are enough reviews with a high-enough average, many readers who care about reviews will take the average at face value and not scrutinize detailed comments.

In other words, not all elements of a retail page are created equally. Choose wisely if you have limited time and funds to invest. New authors in particular often have a hard time deciding whether to invest in paying for critical reviews such as Kirkus or IndieReader. Before you make those sorts of decisions, be aware of elements that are most important and are most visible to readers.

And my final point—my real point—the *trickiest* point of all of this, is the notion that most readers won't get very far before they decide. Readers don't carefully and discerningly read every element of your retail page and make measured decisions about whether to buy. They get only as far as they need to before getting to their personal yes or no. Your non-fiction book may be a treasure-trove of expertly-organized information. Your fiction book may be a literary masterpiece. But if the reader doesn't quickly see enough evidence that they would love your book, they'll abandon your page.

5 BOOK COVERS

LET'S un-learn the adage we were taught in elementary school: people *absolutely* judge books by covers. All of us have been deeply and immediately drawn to books based on their covers alone. Especially in the age of Instagram and YouTube and high-resolution smart phones, people are increasingly visual. We've been conditioned to react to images and we have a lower-than-ever tolerance for reading text. In light of all this, it behooves us to take our book covers very seriously—to understand the out-of-pocket-cost vs. opportunity cost issue.

I meet a lot of authors who don't want to pay more than $50 or $75 per eBook cover. Financially speaking, I understand why. The average indie author makes less than $500 per year—not $500 per book, $500 a year, total. If you're not making very much, but you're shelling out-of-pocket just to get your books out the door, it's hard to justify covers in the $200 or more range (which I believe to be the minimum you'd pay for a highly-professional cover).

But ask yourself this: how many more books would you sell if you had a one-click cover? I didn't coin that term, but I'll bet you know what it means. How many more books would you sell if you had a cover so good that twice the number of people who visited your page chose to buy it? And would the money you made as a result offset the out-of-pocket price you paid to have that supremely-awesome cover designed?

That's what I mean by opportunity cost. By ignoring the revenue you stand to gain from starting with a better cover, you may not be thinking about your start-up costs in a holistic way. Better covers increase conversion rates. Conversion rates are the rate at which people who visit your page tend to buy your book.

A low conversion rate is a sign that your retail page is not performing. If you know how much traffic visited your retail page on a given day and you know how many books you sold that day, you know your conversion rate. For example, if you ran a single ad campaign on Wednesday and you know the ads in that campaign got a total of 100 clicks, however many books you sold divided by 100 is your conversion rate. However, if you typically sell 5 of that book on an average Wednesday when you're not running ad campaigns, you would subtract the baseline of 5 books that you usually sell and divide only the incremental number of books sold by 100.

The point is, the higher your conversion rate, the more you're selling every single day. If better covers will increase your conversion rates, pay the money and have them redesigned.

THE TIME I **Changed My Cover**

When I was gearing up to publish my debut novel, *Snapdragon*, I had a gorgeous cover designed. I'll give you one guess as to the image that showed on front. You guessed right—it was a snapdragon—a pink bloom of the delicate flower. It was pictured against a simple white background with a cool reverse filter effect on my name and the book title, which both appeared in a modern, sans-serif font. The genre of the book was Erotic Romance. I fancied the flower to be cleverly subtle. Everyone will know it's a vagina, I thought, congratulating myself for being so Georgia O'Keefe. The problem was (as I only admitted to myself two weeks before the release after stubbornly holding onto my beautiful cover) that no other authors in Erotic Romance were publishing covers like this.

So I had a choice to make: go with my own artistic vision? Stick with the cover I'd worked so hard with my designer to create, and that I fiercely loved? Or go with a cover I would probably like less but that made the genre clear? Mind you, this was my debut novel. Absolutely nobody knew me. This was my chance to define who I was. The dilemma, of course, was that the flower cover *did* represent me and my writing, which is upmarket compared to most Erotic Romance. It *did* differentiate me and reflect who I was. What I had to come to terms with was the fact that differentiating myself in that way at that stage in my career ran counter to my goals.

So I had another cover designed. This one had nearly-naked people. This one left no question as to whether the genre was Erotic Romance. But I did something else: I made the genre clearer but I made it not-exactly-like-what everyone else was doing. I actually got both—better signaling and effective differentiation. More importantly, I ended up with a cover that does a better job of selling my book. I've seen it in action at signings. People who like the sexy stuff gravitate right to me and my table. My goal was to break out as an author, earn readers and build a fan base from nothing. In order to achieve that within the first year, I had to change my cover.

HOW TO KNOW **When Your Cover Needs Work (i.e., The Value of Honest Friends)**

The first step to auditing your covers is to do some market research. That back and forth I told you I've had with some of my clients? Yeah, it's your turn now. Think through what sub-genre your book needs to align to. Go to your own categories, or, if you're unpublished, the category you would use to file your book. It's super-easy: look for patterns among the books that are trending: do they share similar palettes or color schemes? What about complexity vs. minimalism? Photography vs. Illustrated art? Go to your local bookstore—the bigger the better. Look for books in your own genre. Which books are on display or had their covers turned so they're front-facing? From there, you'll learn what kinds of covers are selling the best. If you really want to sleuth it out, make friends with an actual bookseller. A friend of mine who works for Barnes & Noble always gives me the skinny on which books aren't selling and the ones they box up and send back.

Now, you've come to the hard part: the part where you compare: how well do your own covers align? Do the covers from top-selling books have noticeably-better quality? Does your cover style look dated compared to theirs (e.g., is your cover more like what was common in the genre five years ago, and is it possible that your covers make your book seem less fresh?) Now look at your cover by itself and forget the comparison for a minute: on its own, does your cover correctly signal genre? If it's fiction, does it represent your tropes?

Finally, dig up your most honest friend who also happens to be an author. Someone who's been doing this longer than you. Someone who's been in charge of her own marketing. Bonus points if you find someone who you know can be critical—like your harshest critique partner. Dig up someone who understands publishing and will tell it to you like it is.

If the conclusion you draw is that it's time for a new cover, write down your rationale. For example, if you write Erotic Romance and you've noticed that what's trending right now is no women on book covers, no male faces—just naked male abs, write that down. What I don't want you doing is falling into the trap of shopping for a new cover, getting carried away and picking yet another cover based again on a gut check of what you like. Shop consciously—whether you're shopping for pre-made covers or a designer to make one from scratch. Know what's on your wish list and make sure you get it.

YOUR COVER **vs. Your Goals**

Remember a few chapters ago, when I forced you to write down your goal? Moments like this are exactly why. If you're looking to change your cover—one you may be tethered to by emotion—make your process easier by reminding yourself of what you're trying to do.

Maybe you hate the idea of getting rid of an old cover you love. If your goals aren't to be making a whole lot more money at this, then keep your beloved cover as it is. If all you care about is finding your small, dedicated fan base that totally gets you, your aesthetic, your brand, skip to the next section—your cover is fine. Alternatively, if you said your goal is to make quit-your-day-job money at doing this, you pull every string you can to get the best cover designer in your genre to start taking your calls. Trust me: the authors whose monthly sales would make you green with envy aren't scouring the bargain bin for covers.

6 TITLES AND SUBTITLES

HIGHLY-COMPREHENSIBLE TITLES and subtitles are another way to instantly gain ground with prospects. So are attention-grabbing ones that are memorable but not too weird. Saying right upfront what the book is about orients the reader, saving her from having to scour the blurb to get the basic gist.

Remember: readers' short-term goal is information. They're looking to quickly assess your book and decide whether it's something they'd like. They'll have some modicum of patience for checking you out, but don't overestimate their willingness to keep wading through your retail page until they "get" your book. As the browsing attention span of the average Internet surfer dwindles to nearly nothing, it's wise to make "pithy" your middle name and to make fast comprehension of your retail pages a goal.

I'll admit that literal titles and subtitles make more sense in some genres than others. In literature, you never see subtitles and the more avant garde the main title, the better. As with many opportunities in book marketing, a critical step is to do your research and understand what's selling. If some of the top sellers in your category are using descriptive titles and subtitles, it should serve as pretty good evidence that a critical mass of readers is oriented to thinking in those terms.

WHERE ON-THE-NOSE TITLES AND SUBTITLES WORK BEST

Steven Covey's *The 7 Habits of Highly Effective People* is a great example of a book that lets the title do all the work. You don't need to read the blurb to know that it's a highly-organized self-improvement book that contains seven pieces of tactical advice. Imagine if this book had been called something less specific, like *Musings on Personal Fulfillment* or *How to Win at Life*. The former is boring and, even though the latter is better, what does it even mean?

Beyond non-fiction, which has thrived for years on this level of literality, genre fiction has begun to catch up. It's common to find Cozy Mysteries with titles like *Murder at a Country Inn* or *The Bones He Buried in the Front Yard* and Romance novels with titles like *The Billionaire Sheikh's Secret Twin Babies*. At first glance, titles like these may seem uninspired and even a little lazy. But don't knock them, even if they beat you over the head with the plot.

SEARCHABILITY

What if, in addition to luring prospective readers in through campaign marketing, your books were constantly viewed by new readers who found them on their own? If you choose a title with the kinds of key phrases that your target reader might search on, you'll drive new users to your page for free.

I got my second-best pre-release sales on the first book I ever tried this strategy with. Before I announced this book release in my newsletter and within hours of going live on Amazon, it started racking up sales. The main title—*Crazy Old Money*—was a deliberate word play on *Crazy Rich Asians*. The tropes in the two books are similar and, once you get it, the reference is kind of cute, but it's not the kind of main title that magnets readers.

Enter my subtitle. I wanted to capture readers who were searching for a Romantic Comedy. I also wanted them to know that my story starred an interracial couple and involved a billionaire. There's coded language that readers use in the Romance genre to look for pairings between an African-American heroine and a white hero: the keyword is BWWM (Black Woman White Man). The full title and subtitle I went with is *Crazy Old Money: A BWWM Billionaire Romantic Comedy*.

I didn't just trust my gut about which keywords to put into the subtitle. I researched several keywords I was considering, to look at which ones got the most traffic. I could have gone with "interracial" instead of "BWWM" to describe my romantic pairing, but "BWWM" gets a lot more monthly Amazon searches. I could have tried "A BWWM Romantic Comedy about Rich People" but the word "billionaire" is used more frequently in Romance as a signal that a main character is wealthy. Going with the commonly-used "billionaire" had the best shot at connecting with my reader and signaling appropriately about my book.

STRATEGIC **Execution**

If you're sold on the idea of being Captain Obvious, here are four steps you can take to get to a title that will boost your discoverability and conversion rates:

1. **Brainstorm** a concise list of keywords that get to the heart of your book's narrative. In non-fiction, look at the core value of the information conveyed. In fiction, look at themes and tropes. Any element that is

hot and trending in the market, and any tidbit that might give your book an advantage should be considered at this stage.

2. **Research** the keywords you're looking at. This is hard to do without a tool like KDP Rocket, which gives you search engine statistics from Amazon. Your goal here—whatever tool you use—is to find out how many readers are already searching on a buzz word you're considering. Keywords that are highly-applicable to your book and get the highest search volume, win.

3. **Try out** complete subtitles with keywords that sound like they could be winners. Come up with a few phrases based on a few finalists that sound like they might work. Find a test group—this may be other authors who have wisdom about such things, or maybe even your own readers depending on how this aligns to your existing library. Find people who are as familiar as possible with what you're trying to do to weigh in on your plan.

4. **Decide** on something that strikes the right balance between getting a ton of searches and having the best ring to it. Both will be important in selling books.

Final note: subtitles are somewhat flexible. On most retailer sites, you can change subtitles as fluidly as you want to. Don't abuse it, but know that, as far as most eBook retailers are concerned, subtitles aren't set in stone.

7 REVIEWS

A POPULAR LIE that I hear sometimes from authors is that readers don't care about reviews. That "everyone knows five-star reviews are fake" and "one-star reviews are trolls" is baseless speculation. Dynamics (and drama) that authors are well-aware of— everything from buying reviews to Amazon's pesky habit of removing many legitimate ones—are issues that most readers aren't following. If you've been in the publishing world for long enough, you know that authors have a lot of baggage when it comes to this issue—not only about how important reviews may be, but around whether and how to pursue getting more.

I won't delve into a point-by-point indictment of why I am 100% sure that reviews matter to most readers, even if caring about reviews only boils down to a cursory glance. What I will point to instead is evidence that, as a society, we are conditioned to care about what our peers think when it comes to nearly every kind of product— not just books. This is called social proof. It's been studied extensively in the broader business and product marketing world and, google the research—it matters.

Let's say you're on Amazon to buy something like a charging

cable to run from your laptop to your phone. Charging cables are basically a commoditized product. Some of them look a bit flashier than others, but they seem similar on the surface and they're also similarly-priced. How do you decide which charging cable to buy? Chances are, you read the reviews. You pay attention to how many reviews there are, how positive they are, and you may even read some of the most positive and negative accounts.

The key concept here is the commodity. If you're looking at a commoditized product—a product that may be sold by many vendors but that is difficult to distinguish from similar products—you may need to look deeper for distinguishing characteristics or quality. Books are a commoditized product. We don't like to say that they are, but they are. The market for literature is saturated and readers can decreasingly tell one product from another. For this reason, I view reviews as more important than ever, particularly if you're writing in a very crowded space. Because readers have choices, they will look for distinguishing characteristics.

I've seen this proven out in my own conversion rates and in the conversion rates of my clients. My books with the most reviews convert the best. My books with a 4.5-star rating convert better than those with a 4.0-star rating. And on retailers where I don't have very many reviews at all, my conversion rates are weak.

You can transcend this if you are writing a book in a super-hot and trending space, but that won't be the case for most authors, and it certainly won't be the case all the time. My personal policy is to not spend advertising dollars on a book that doesn't have enough positive reviews to strengthen the reader's propensity to convert. The number of reviews one "needs" is a matter of opinion. For me, this number is fifty.

· · ·

HOW TO GET MORE **Reviews from Existing Readers**

Along the lines of readers not being privy to the review drama that goes on in the authoring world, so also are they not-that-aware of how important reviews are to authors. Naturally-critical and, dare I say, self-important types gravitate toward wanting to give their $0.02 whether you ask them to or not. But many readers—often the most satisfied ones—view themselves as insignificant to the process.

Changing this self-perception requires training. If you have direct access to your reader base (as you would with a mailing list), you have to ask for reviews. Readers who love your work will *want* to help you in this way, but they can't respond to what you haven't asked.

You don't have to beg or reek of desperation as you do it, but you do have to be humble. Make a case for why reviews are important to authors without being condescending. I always take the time to underscore that I would love an *honest* review. I'm weirdly-proud of the fact that my most loyal super-fans don't five-star me every time. Real relationships are honest ones. Be honest with your fans about your need for reviews and encourage them to be honest about your books.

There are other strategies for how to cultivate a loyal, consistent stream of reviews from your direct-access reader base, most of which are too involved to cover in a single chapter and some of which are highly dependent on career stage and the health of your fan base. I've dedicated a separate marketing guide to the topic of reviews. Overall, the rule is to ask for what you need and to find fun, creative, incentive-filled ways to do it.

HOW TO GET MORE **Reviews from Strangers**

If you're still building your fan base, or are simply going for more reviews, plenty of review services, such as Net Galley,

Booksprout, and Hidden Gems will pony up reviewers for a fee. The topic of "paying" for reviews is also too extensive to cover in a single chapter. But I can be clear about one thing: Amazon doesn't allow authors to commission guaranteed reviews. There can be no tit-for-tat relationship or obligation.

In that sense, what these services are doing is investing in building their own follower bases and charging you to gain access to readers who have been vetted for interest in reviewing. In some cases, these readers have shown a track record of leaving reviews. If you go through one of these services and authorize the distribution of 100 review copies, you won't get 100 reviews, but the better services have yield rates of 80% to 90% and they remove readers from their list who don't demonstrate that they're actively reviewing.

These are not the same as fraudulent services that use fake readers to plant five-star reviews (which would, again, violate Amazon's terms). In fact, it's common for readers to be disappointed by how low their star ratings are from review services like the three listed above. The reviewers are real readers. Even though you're giving them something for free, they're using hours of their time to read your book. If they dislike it, they either won't leave a review or they'll let you know with a lower rating.

I find that review services are great to use when you're confident in the quality of your writing and when your book aligns very clearly to a single genre. And services such as these aren't just for new releases or Advance Reader Copies (ARCs). These services work just fine if your backlist needs more reviews.

WHEN POSITIVE REVIEWS **are a Problem**

If you have a good number of reviews but the average rating is low, it's worth getting an opinion from three professional beta readers who are familiar with your genre. Unlike a developmental editor, who would write extensive notes on issues with the story arc or narrative flow, or a copy editor, who would go through and fix style issues, a professional beta reader would summarize strengths and weaknesses through a reader's lens. This assessment should comment not only on the content of the story, but also on whether the story delivers on its promise (e.g., what is signaled by the title, cover and blurb). Hiring three will allow you to see where the feedback is unanimous, lowering the risk that you make changes based on any one person's tastes. It will also ensure that you receive organized, honest feedback (as opposed to asking for beta reads from author friends).

Even if you don't hope to market poorly-reviewed books aggressively, they can negatively impact your brand. It's not uncommon for self-published authors to pull down titles that aren't showing well, and to re-release them later after they'd been revamped.

Along those lines, if there is reasonable consensus that your book has problems, don't spend money advertising. It's not worth it to earn new readers if the book in question can't convert them into fans. Fix the book itself, get the retail page healthy, and go from there. If necessary, pull together an ARC team to jump-start a new wave of reviews.

EDITORIAL REVIEWS **and Endorsements**

Even well-known authors gather editorial reviews and endorsements from trusted sources. Unlike reader reviews, these show that an authority with taste and credibility can vouch for your book. If you're traditionally-published, chances are that your publisher is drumming up editorial reviews on your behalf. If they've taken your book on a press tour, they may be gathering quoted endorsement from bloggers.

But if you're indie-published, the onus is on you to drum up reviews from credible sources. Unless you're a very big (or very well-funded) indie, these can be hard to get. For starters, there's an entire industry that charges for editorial reviews. Recognizable ones, such as Kirkus, Clarion and IndieReader, charge between $250 and $550. They can take up to 9 weeks and what you receive in return isn't always great. Even if a reviewer loved your book, the praise can lack the elegance you would want for retail pages and ads. A common complaint is that reviewers are sometimes lazy: going light on actual opinion commentary and instead merely summarizing the book.

It's possible to earn free editorial reviews, but this typically involves a query-like process: you submit your upcoming title at least 4 months in advance of the release date and it will be considered for a review. These free review programs are very competitive for indie authors, but if you've got the patience to sit on your manuscript for a few months before publishing, magazines like Foreword Indie and Publisher's Weekly (through Book-Life) take submissions.

Endorsements from authors and bloggers is simply about getting someone big to blurb your book. Here, "big" is used as a relative term. Any author with a serious credibility (such as bestseller status), and any influencer with a loud microphone and a dedicated following, will do.

Since editorial reviews appear below-the-fold, I don't consider them to be of utmost importance. Pursue them, but don't put them first. Particularly if you're thinking of paying for reviews, make sure there's no other area of your marketing plan that could use that money more.

8 BLURBS

MANY OF THE same principles that apply to titles and subtitles also apply to blurbs. Only, blurbs require a lot more elegance and finesse. The best ones go far beyond dumping information—they excite and inspire around a promise, dangling candy that the reader can't resist.

Though the building blocks of strong blurbs are similar to those used to construct highly-marketable titles, execution is more advanced. Norms around structure and point-of-view pivot on genre. For example, there is a current trend, in some genre fiction, to write blurbs in first person. Understanding what blurb structure is working in the current marketplace for books that align to yours is important research.

Beyond emphasizing the importance of research, this chapter will dive into reader psychology, give a killer testing tip, and deconstruct common mistakes. It will also discuss how to hire someone to write them for you if blurb-writing isn't your forte.

.   .   .

WHAT BLURBS ARE REALLY ABOUT

It's hard to talk about blurbs without starting again with the deepest desire of the reader. I'll risk beating a dead horse if it means impressing the following upon you:

- Readers want to understand your book in as little time and with as little effort as possible
- Their goal is to quickly decide whether your book seems good enough to buy
- If they're bored, confused, or overwhelmed by what you're showing them, they will abandon your page and not buy your book
- Your job is to make every element on the page strengthen your reader's intention to buy

Blurb-writing is about one thing and one-thing only: leaving a trail of breadcrumbs so sweet that the reader can't help but to follow them to the cake. It really is that easy: give your reader a taste of something they know that they absolutely love, and you'll be successful in selling them the book.

So, what do readers know they love? In fiction, readers know they love certain tropes. They know they love themes, time periods and settings. Bringing up certain character archetypes also works. Your blurb should show off aspects of your world and elements of your story that readers will love to escape into: bait them with a small town, a meddling mother-in-law, a crushing secret, or a haunted house. I know at least a dozen people (myself included) who go absolutely bananas for a story with a dog.

In non-fiction, the bait is more about style. Is a true crime story gripping? Is it fast-paced or so deeply exploratory that it takes its time? Is a how-to book expository and descriptive, or is it conveniently organized into bullets? Blurb-writing is less about describing the content of the book than it is about cluing the reader into whether she's going to love it.

WHAT **Not to Do**

- **Don't summarize.** I know this sounds counterintuitive. Summarizing your book is a huge mistake. Your reader doesn't need to know everything that happens in your book—she just needs to know enough to know whether she'll like it. Your blurb should be packed with selling points that will sway your target audience—nothing more.
- **Don't be tied to chronology or linearity.** You don't have to start at the beginning or reach a certain point in your narrative, let alone reach the end. The exception may be advice-based literature, for which readers may want to know exactly what will be covered and exactly how that information may be laid out. For most other book types, it's not that important to be linear.
- **Don't be loath to give up the plot or other big information.** Particularly in fiction, many authors don't want to give up a big plot reveal. They want the reader to be surprised. The problem is, the kind of surprise that awaits the reader may be a huge selling point. What if a secret twin is behind wrongdoing in a Suspense Thriller? What if someone faked her own death in a Cozy Mystery? What if a married protagonist is secretly in love with her best friend in a Romance? Secret twin, faked death, and best-friends-to-lovers are all tropes that some readers

will love. You will sell more books if you hint in the blurb exactly-what-juicy-reader-favorite trope will probably happen. If you don't want to give a huge spoiler, go for innuendo without being too vague. And give your reader some credit—savvy readers are there for the journey and know what's going to happen anyway.

TESTING YOUR BLURB

It's difficult to judge the appeal of your own blurb, especially if you're the one who wrote it. Even if you're not, a little testing goes a long, long way. Your ability to test, of course, depends on your circumstances. If you're indie and in control of all of your marketing assets, testing as described here is a viable approach. All you need is creative content for an ad and a plan for a landing page. Here's what you can do:

- **Create blurb variations.** Write (or have written) at least two variations of your blurb and develop a logic for what you are testing. You may write two blurbs describing identical content that vary widely in tone. Conversely, you may write two blurbs in the same tone and test the appeal of different information about your book.
- **Create a Facebook ad.** Use your book cover or a stock image that fits your book to create a high-quality ad image. Then, in the copy section of each ad, switch in each variation of your blurb. This trick is widely used in the digital advertising industry: testing how well certain messages play based purely on an ad click-through rate.

- **Create a landing page scheme.** If your book is released or available for pre-order, the ad should link to your retail page. If it does, you have an opportunity to measure conversions. The tricky thing here is that, while different ad variations may contain different blurbs, your retail page can only contain one blurb at a time. For that reason, you may have to run ad campaigns testing blurb copy sequentially so that you can see not only click-through rates but conversion rates for a given blurb. If your book has no retail page, you could create landing pages that align to each ad message and use a call-to-action like a sign-up for an alert for when the title is released.

- **Analyze results.** Figure out which blurbs earned the highest click-through rates, and, from there, find out which ones yielded the best conversions. Hard and soft conversions both count. If your book is released or available for pre-order, the hard conversion is a sale. If your book isn't yet released, the soft conversion is the rate at which users bit on the call to action. By running a controlled experiment, with variations happening the same number of days and days of the week (in the event that you can't run tests in parallel), patterns will emerge.

HOW TO HIRE **a Blurb Writer**

If you're not a great blurb writer, hire a professional. There are writers who rock at this. I've seen blurb writers charge everything from $50 to $250 per blurb and take everywhere from a few days to several weeks to get you a draft. Unlike editing, which is a mature, structured field, professional blurb writing feels younger and less organized. There is no standard process all blurb writers follow, no common set of inputs you might be asked for, and no single philosophy that all of them adhere to in terms of what works.

In my experience, there's no correlation between how long a blurb-writer takes, what she charges, and the quality of the end product. I also find that you can still "hear" the distinctive voice of the writer, even if they make adjustments to align to your work. Unless you're so bad at writing blurbs that nearly anything will be better than what you could do yourself, it may take some real looking before you find a blurb writer who is right for you.

It's good to look to blurb writers with experience in your genre. I've almost always gotten the worst results from generalists. Any experienced blurb writer will have a before vs. after portfolio. Since most blurb writers don't only write new blurbs from scratch—they take older blurbs and give them a good fix—the before vs. after perspective is a great indicator of their capabilities.

Some blurb writers advertise on their blurbs' ability to sell books and want you to focus on book sales for the blurbs they've written. I don't think that apparent book sales or rankings are an indicator of a blurb's effectiveness. Because books are at different ages and stages, and because different advertising efforts may be underway for individual books, it's hard to comment or compare what a blurb alone is doing for sales performance.

OTHER ALTERNATIVES

A common problem in hiring blurb writers is that, no matter how valiant their efforts to understand your book, they still haven't read it. If you work with critique partners or editors or any other industry professional who has read your book and knows what blurbs are all about, hiring one of them to take on your blurb—or to at least assist—may be your best bet. In my experience, those who don't like or aren't good at blurb writing simply won't take them on. Conversely, a skilled wordsmith who thoroughly understands the work in question often does the best job.

9 PRICING

PRICING IS a fascinating discipline that's become more complicated in the world of publishing. Until ten or fifteen years ago, readers had a good sense for what a book was "worth". Thanks to the big, traditional publishers, who owned mass markets for decades and set fairly standard pricing, books were sold as items of value, even where there were low-cost alternatives (e.g., the pocket versions seen in airports and supermarkets).

Alternative pricing models such as Kindle Unlimited, free eBooks across major distributors, and subscription services have created advantages for readers but complicated things for authors. You'll sell more books if your titles are priced correctly for your genre and your brand, though, given these new complexities, let's explore what's relevant, now:

- **Genre norms.** Most readers arrive at retail pages with a point of view on typical prices within the genre. It matters what other authors are charging for similar content. If your work strays too far in either direction from the norm, it will be more difficult to sell your book.

- **Brand perceptions.** Some authors have premium brands. If you are a household name like Nora Roberts, James Patterson or Stephen King, what you charge for a single book may never be questioned. Even if a reader has never heard of you, a retail page full of strong reviews, a great cover and blurb, and all the things that have been covered previously around making a good show will boost your perceived brand value.

- **Perceived competitive value for full-priced books.** Does your book show much better (or much worse) than comparable genre examples? Readers care about how good your book looks for the price. If your book shows worse than your comparables, readers may not be willing to pay even the genre standard.

- **Perceived value at a time of subscriptions and freebies.** I'll say it plainly: if you write in a genre in which a lot of authors are using Kindle Unlimited or another deep-discount subscription service, you're at a disadvantage. Services like these train readers to believe that books are a nearly worthless, renewable commodity. Dynamics like these impact everyone, from debut authors to seasoned bestsellers. If readers in your genre have come to expect books to be very cheap, or to seem like they're free, your book will have a hard time competing unless you're participating in said services and pricing accordingly, or unless the justification for your premium pricing is clear. I cringe to even use the word "premium" but if readers perceive that your book is more expensive than most of what they're seeing, they'll want supporting evidence to be convinced that your book merits a higher price.

- **Ability to pay.** The socioeconomic status of your target reader should factor in as well. Certain genres, such as Women's Fiction, charge higher prices for books because they're known to attract a reader base with above-average income. For a voracious reader without a lot of disposable income, $3.99 is a lot of money to pay for a single book. Sustaining a 15-book a month habit at this price point adds up to ~$60 a month. Some readers who use subscription services aren't just looking to get a great deal—they simply can't afford to pay beyond a certain amount on their reading habit each month. If you suspect that one of your books is targeted to a demographic that can't afford to buy at a certain price point, that should factor into your pricing decision and profitability model.

TRADEOFFS AND COMMON MISTAKES

The biggest mistake I see on retail pages is overpricing on books that don't show well. Brand new, self-published authors sometimes make this mistake. And I understand the mistake—the temptation to price higher comes from a desire to earn a decent royalty off of every unit sold. The logic is that higher prices = more royalties = more money. This logic ignores that you might make more money, even at a lower royalty level, by selling a greater number of books.

Overpricing isn't limited to self-published authors. Traditional publishers overprice, too, for reasons that are more complicated. For one, the traditional publishing industry doesn't want to be complicit in the devaluing of books. If traditional publishers lowered their prices, it would narrow the range and further convince the reader base that books just aren't worth very much. As a result, however, some traditionally-published books don't do as well as they could because they're at prices that can't compete with high-quality, lower-cost competitors.

A New York Times Bestseller List-topping friend of mine confided that she fought her publisher tooth-and-nail to lower the price of the first book in her big series. Her hypothesis was that she could earn so many new readers by making it affordable to try this first book, that she would make up the lost revenue from book one royalties on the back end. After months of back and forth my friend wore her publisher down and got them to acquiesce to trying her approach. To the publisher's surprise, my friend was right: the strategy multiplied sales for book one, but earned a new reader base that was willing and able to pay full price for subsequent books.

Underpricing is also an issue—I'm not talking about promotional discounts or strategically-executed freebies—I'm talking about permanent prices that are simply too low. I'm sure you've heard the saying, "you get what you pay for". This kind of thinking explains why higher pricing is sometimes viewed as an indicator of higher quality. Along the same lines, when people see something that is priced lower-than-expected, they may think the opposite.

DISCOUNTS AND FREEBIES
Overall, *The Book Marketing Audit* is designed to speak to permanent, every day strategies for your book's retail page. Since

your goal should be to earn full-price royalties on as many books as possible, I don't recommend using freebies and discounts widely. The argument against them is that, by giving too much away, you're attracting the wrong kind of reader. Most of us prefer readers with a desire to pay the asking price or the subscription price over those out for a free lunch.

Still, there is broad wisdom around discounts and freebies that applies to permanent pricing. If you have a large-enough library (and particularly if you write series), throwing out free or discounted "book bait" to usher new readers into your ecosystem tends to pay off.

10 CONNECTING THE DOTS

THERE ARE a few topics that have nothing to do with retail pages that still tie to the strength of your marketing game. The audit process is designed to force you to look at these elements—to catch other areas where you may be squandering opportunities to build a more solid marketing foundation and sell more books.

BACK MATTER

I get it. It's easy to publish a book, then kind of forget about it. We do the best we can with back matter around the original publication date. Then, things change. Our library grows. So does our author infrastructure. We have different things to say about ourselves and our library than we did yesteryear. Given developments like these, shouldn't our back matter change with us?

The answer—clearly—is yes. But back matter is one of those things that authors really don't like to go back and change. It's tedious. And if we had a formatter or a publisher deal with our earlier back matter, we now have to go back and negotiate or figure out how to keep it updated moving forward. But, folks...

back matter is low-hanging fruit. If you go back in your library and bring all of your back matter up-to-date, you'll sell more books based on this better explanation of your library, alone.

Here are the kinds of things you should be doing as you go through and update your back matter:

- Add new books you've written to your "Also By" page.
- Refresh your author biography.
- Make your links custom tracking links so that you can monitor where you're getting clicks on your back matter material. On any platform, these can be as simple as bit.ly links, or, on Amazon, you could do an affiliate program custom link.
- Since Amazon funnels Kindle readers right back into the store before taking readers to your back matter, integrate the best practice of embedding links to new books into the final chapter.

Finally, as your library grows, you may want to alter how you're stepping your readers through your titles. When my library was smaller, the back matter of each book linked to each upcoming release. Now that I've reached the ten-book mark, more sensible groupings have taken shape and it no longer makes sense to link my books chronologically. Revamping your back matter will force you to think strategically around how to transition your readers from book-to-book.

FAN OWNERSHIP

Another thing you should consider before you step up your marketing game is to make sure you're set up to know and retain your own fans. This usually means making sure you have your own newsletter. I know that some authors hate the idea of maintaining one and have no idea what they'd say or how frequently they'd send anything out, but it's a huge advantage to be able to connect with your own fans on your own terms.

Here's what I mean by that: it's great if you have 10,000 Facebook followers to your fan group or fan page, but let's say that Facebook goes out of business tomorrow, or does something far more likely, such as lose your data or suspend your account. It would be impossible for you to reconnect with those fans because you never really had full access to them—Facebook was providing that access to you.

One of the smartest moves you can make in this business is to make sure that nobody other than you owns the relationship with your fans. Not Facebook. Not Amazon. Not Bookbub. Not any platform where fans have to go through someone else to follow you. It's fine to build followings on those platforms, but you need a way to directly connect with your base. Before you go hard on finding more readers, make sure you have in place a way to capture direct contact information of fans who are actively in your orbit. This includes everything from newsletter sign-ups, to ARC readers you connect with via Instafreebie or Bookfunnel, and even old-fashioned "join my mailing list" forms you put on your table at book signings.

TRACKING INFRASTRUCTURE

All marketing hinges on learning and you can't learn if you're not tracking. Getting in good shape from a tracking perspective resolves the following questions:

- How many people who read my eBooks click on a link in the back and buy the next book?

- Which books garner the most interest with respect to teasers?
- How many people are visiting my website, and what pages are of most interest to them?
- Which elements of my newsletter are my fans most likely to click on?
- Can I leverage people who visit my website for certain kinds of advertising? (e.g. Facebook custom audiences)

Unless you have web development experience, hire a professional to put this infrastructure in place. You'll want to do things like add Google Analytics tracking code to your web pages, add Google and Facebook pixels to your website, do some custom configuration with Google Tag Manager, add tracking mechanisms to your newsletter, and do some quality testing to make sure everything's tracking through.

Using affiliate links as a hack to better-understand conversions compensates for the fact that you don't have the benefit of receiving direct conversion data from retail sites. Custom-configuring affiliate links (especially on Amazon) will tell you even more about what prospective readers are browsing and buying.

Even if you don't feel ready for this level of detail, it won't hurt you to set up the infrastructure. One day, the stronger your marketing game becomes, either you or a professional marketer you hire, will care a lot about the data.

It's not worth it to go big on a new marketing plan if you haven't covered pieces like this. You don't just want to do more—you want to be as smart as possible and put your best foot forward. There's no sense in making big improvements if you're just going to let little things obscure your potential and shoot you in the foot. Clean your house and handle what you need to, to bolster your success.

11 ADD IT UP

ONLY ONCE YOU'VE looked at your retail pages, stepped up your quality so that all is what it should be and made sure that your books can convert, both from the initial sale and through the back matter, are you ready to take the final step—a step that many people come into this thinking is the first step. Only now that you're polished and shiny and in your best possible position to convert prospective readers at a high rate are you ready to drive traffic to your books and your brand.

So, let's go back to this "one size doesn't fit all" concept. Even if your retail pages are now lovely, that doesn't mean that your tactical marketing mix should be identical to that of other authors you know. This chapter breaks down individual tactics and comments on what kind of authors and libraries said tactics are good for vs. what kinds of authors and libraries should leave them alone.

A WORLD **of Marketing Tactics**

First things first: this list of marketing tactics isn't comprehensive. It's directional in nature and comments on whether these highly-popular and much-talked about channels are appropriate to your career stage, library and brand. This is high-level commentary designed to help you avoid mistakes and uncover opportunities. It's largely based on the most common questions and missteps I see authors make.

- **Street Teams.** Street teams are groups of readers who authors recruit to become their regular Advance Reader Copy (ARC) reviewers. These are readers who you gather organically, or possibly through the use of a Promoting Personal Assistant (PPA). These readers may be new to you and be simply willing to review books in a genre they love, or they may be super-fans who follow your books and your career. If you're an established author, you probably have something that resembles a street team, regardless of what you call it. If you're new, and particularly if you don't have many reviews, I do recommend trying to build such a team as early as possible in your career. I have around 30 street team reviewers who have been loyal to me since my very first novel and they come in right on time when I do a new release and want early reviews. Also, since long-term street team members turn out to be super-fans, building and getting to know your tribe is a lot of fun!

- **Newsletter Swaps.** Finding authors who are similar to you in genre and in follower volume may be strong partners. However, not all newsletter swaps are created equally. Some authors who do newsletter swaps are featuring ten or more other authors in their newsletter at one time. It's not a great proposition for you if your book's visibility is likely to be buried.

Also, it's important to check out your own moral compass. Adding other authors' books to your newsletters is basically endorsing those authors and books. You will lose trust with your readers if you "recommend" books that are low-quality, books that aren't like yours, or books with questionable themes or elements that they might truly hate. Your readers are trusting you not to use them as marketing pawns. If you do newsletter swaps, I recommend screening the books and the authors you're considering partnering with. If the books you feature truly are a good fit for your readers, everybody wins.

- **Social Media.** This is a big topic and I tackle it fully in a separate marketing guide. The main thing to know about social media is that it's not a great direct sales channel for books, but it will solidify your relationship with fans and build your brand. Just because you tweet that you have a new release doesn't mean that tweet will yield sales. However, if you use social media as a place to share your successes, communicate with those in your community, and build a likable persona, people will feel connected to you and will be more invested in your success. I would say that social media is a must for authors who care a lot about fan relationships and for authors who want to sell very big over the long-term. The bigger you want to go, the more likely you'll reach a point that you need to compel readers to act. If you've nurtured relationships, you'll be in a good position to ask.

- **Blog Tours.** I don't love blog tours for sales. I don't think that most blogs command a follower base well enough to move the needle. Bloggers have also gotten lazy about using real reviews (as opposed to regurgitated ones provided by PR companies). There are some huge blogs, but many of those are in bed with book promotion services and the traditional PR engine. It's difficult to get the attention of the better ones that aren't. While I don't think they're cost-effective for most authors, there are certain goals (e.g., reaching bestseller status on a list) that require authors who want said goal to make sure their book is everywhere readers turn during a concentrated promotion period. For the average author who's still trying to achieve basic profitability, I tend to think there are better ways to spend your money.

- **Automated Ad Platforms.** The Facebooks and Amazon Marketing Services (AMS) of the world can work well for books that show well. Again, don't use these until your retail pages can convert. Facebook has more features, better targeting and much larger scale. The complaint of AMS is that CPCs (Costs per Click) are too expensive. Depending on the economics of your click costs (which comes down to how competitive your genre is), this tactic will pay off much better if you have more titles released and better sell-through potential for your books.

- **Promotion Sites and E-mail Services.** I'm thinking of sites like Bookbub, Bargain Booksy, Robin Reads, and other promotion services that send out genre-specific recommendations to their readers. Promotion sites charge anywhere from $20 per promotion to $1,500 per promotion (clearly, the latter example is Bookbub). Most promotion sites are hit or miss, mainly because you never know whether your book will be featured nearer to the top or the bottom of the list. You'll get the best ROI out of these services if (again) your retail pages show well, you discount to an attractive price during your promotion, and your book cover is better-than-average for your genre. For the better ones (like Bookbub and Robin Reads) you may sell enough books to earn out the money you spent on the promotion on day one. Be willing to take a loss if the book you promote will lead to sell-through in your library.

- **Personal Appearances.** Signings and conferences are extremely expensive and results can be hit or miss. If you've paid for airfare and hotel out of your own pocket, you need to sell hundreds of books to make back your investment. On one hand, print books have much higher margins, and you might make a good $6 or $7 in royalties for each book. Still, that may mean you need to sell 200 books to offset your cost, and most authors don't sell that many books at most conferences. This is where understanding your goal is important. If you like canoodling with fans, attend these kinds of events. Admirers who feel that they know you and have made a real connection with you are likely to be loyal to you, for longer. They will evangelize you. They'll tell their friends they met you. They'll be your biggest fans. The other thing to consider when it comes to deciding about signings is that you'll meet other authors, and that big bloggers sometimes come to these events. Get the most out of these opportunities by networking. For all you know, the gal you laughed it up with at the bar last night is a colossally huge podcaster and she'll mention you on her next episode. If you discover another author whose books are like yours, you may have just found your next newsletter swap partner or made a friend who wants to interview you for her blog. In my experience, these sorts of events (in addition to being loads of fun, because you can't spend every day in your bath robe writing) carry intangible benefits that always pay off.

ADVICE FOR DEBUT AUTHORS

If you're just starting out, your focus should be on growing your fan base and building a brand. This means you're going to need readers. At this point in your career, when nobody knows you, you have no strong track record or any compelling reason why readers might want to look at your books, it's fine to find early readers by using freebies.

I don't recommend giving your book out for free on a large scale, and certainly not an unsecured one—avoid making your full, finished book available in manuscript form (because, pirating!) What I do recommend is pulling together a street team of folks who read in your genre and would be willing to review your book in exchange for an advance reader copy (ARC). Build until you have a critical mass of positive reviews. Showing a well-received first release will add credibility when it's time to release a second book.

The second thing that new and debut authors can jump on are ad opportunities that focus on new releases. Typically, readers understand that if they see an ad for a book on release day, or even during release week, that a lack of reviews isn't a bad signal. Some promotion services, like Written Word Media's NewinBooks feature, focuses on these. Also, bloggers love new releases. Particularly if nobody knows who you are yet and you want something other than your website to come up when someone Googles your author name, create more searchability on your author brand by pursuing a blog tour.

As I said earlier, it's very difficult to be profitable when you've only released a single title. Unless you're making more than $3.00 or $4.00 in royalties for each book, the cost of acquiring a new reader may be higher than the royalties from selling a single book. If you're a debut author, focus on showing well on that first book and diligently keep writing. You'll be more profitable once you release that second book.

ADVICE FOR AUTHORS **with Small Libraries**

If you have a small library, steady-state tactics like platform advertising and paid promotions are appropriate. If you have strong sell-through on two-to-three titles, you can earn new readers through advertising, and do so at a profit. Your focus has to be amplification. Your book can sell, but you're only scratching the surface when it comes to new readers, so get it in front of the right audiences and start to build your base.

If you don't quite have a large-enough number of books or strong-enough sell-through rates to be sustainable, you must decide whether to earn as many new readers as possible at a thin profit or at a loss or whether to earn only as many readers as you can, profitably. Your situation will improve once you have more books in your library (and, if sell-through is really an issue, once you address that element). If your budget is tight, it's a viable strategy to stay thin on marketing until you have more books released.

ADVICE FOR AUTHORS **with Large Libraries**

If you have a large library, the best piece of advice is to find your strongest "funnel" books—these are books that are most conducive to getting readers to read through multiple titles. If it seems daunting to go back and "fix" every single retail page (a complain that I've heard before), prioritize fixing those titles that you'll use to funnel new readers into your system. With a large library, you are in the strongest position to be profitable in this business. In fact, if you have 10+ titles and aren't making money, something about your ecosystem is wrong. Either your retail pages aren't showing well enough or your book content isn't strong enough to turn a single reader into a repeat reader. If you aren't getting strong sell-through consider hiring a professional and re-editing your books.

ADVICE FOR AUTHORS **with New Releases**

Regardless of library size, if you're planning a new release, there are certain opportunities that are unique to this event. Bloggers usually prefer to write about new titles. In fact, most everybody in your reader world, whether they're social followers, newsletter fans or friends and family, will be compelled to check out something that is brand new. Nearly as exciting as the release itself is the hype that builds up to it—new releases provide opportunities to create anticipation. There are wonderful lists, guides and courses available for how to plan an effective release. The best advice for today's market goes far beyond cover reveals, Facebook parties, and takeovers. You can fall back on ads and other steady-state tactics until the end of time, but you only get to do each release once. Milk it for everything it's worth.

ADVICE FOR AUTHORS **with Varied Libraries**

If you write across genres and/or write a lot of standalones and you don't have direct series linkages to fall back on, for the purposes of marketing, do deep thinking about your brand. For example, I write in at least four sub-genres of romance and I also write Women's Fiction, a fact that could be a disaster. But it's not a disaster, because I realized that feminist fiction is my brand. If your library is varied, readers will need help to understand your offerings and you will need to take steps to help them along. I may never write the same sub-genres and tropes, but my readers know that I always have strong, empowered heroines. Plenty of my fans have read across my entire library because, for them, the feminist fiction angle is enough.

PART 3
GET IT DONE

12 GET IT DONE

HAVING A MORE solid plan feels good, doesn't it? What feels a heck of a lot less good is having to execute it. I'd be a first-class jerk if I gave all the good advice about what to do without any tips and tricks for how to get it done. In an earlier section of this book, I made a case for the importance of quality in marketing. This final section is designed to help you manage the quality of your marketing execution as well as your time.

I won't pretend that a lot of the advice in this section will be easy to take. The idea of doing marketing correctly is daunting, and we all just want things to be simple. But, just as you wouldn't entrust your children or your parents or your pet to any caregiver, so also can you not entrust just any caregiver to your career and your brand.

WHAT YOU CAN STOP DOING

Before you look at managing what new things might fall on your plate, let's go back to your limits. If you discovered that you really *don't* want to be spending five hours a week on social media or that you'd like to shift your limited time and energy from newsletters to ad campaigns, it's time to scale a few things down.

There are steps to doing this right: communicating necessary changes to your fan base and unwinding any supports. If it's going to seem like you're around less, or like you've packed up and started hanging out in a different place, give your fans a head's up. Maybe you decided to reallocate your conference budget to Facebook campaigns, or that you'll step back from Twitter in order to go full-force on Instagram. Let fans know the new best place to find you. Better yet, position it as a positive change and drum up enthusiasm around having them engage you there.

On the support end, there's good news: if you were paying for software (or people) to help you in areas you're shifting away from, cancel your subscriptions and rework your arrangements. Maybe you can downgrade from a paid version of your e-mail software to a free one if you'll be sending messages less frequently. Maybe you can cancel your social media scheduling software altogether.

My hope for you is that letting go feels good—that it tastes like empowerment. Don't dwell on something you've spent far-too-long on and chide yourself for failure. Marketing *is* failing. You have to fail in order to learn, and you have to learn in order to optimize. Let's close the page on the last chapter of your marketing journey and let a new one begin.

13 DIY

DO YOU REMEMBER THE "SCARED STRAIGHT" questions I asked you at the beginning of the book? About how many hours a week you're really willing to spend on marketing? Whether you're willing to gain professional-level proficiency in any area that you plan to take on? Whether, realistically, everything you should be executing as part of your plan is something you have the capacity to learn to do well yourself? Honesty here is important. Ideally, you're arriving to this chapter with a split list of things you can and should be doing yourself and things you'll need a professional to tackle.

There's a reason why companies hire marketing agencies. Marketing agencies have different departments to represent different skills. The department that writes copy and does graphics (usually, the creative department) has nothing to do with the department that runs campaigns. So, be realistic about what you can't—and maybe even shouldn't—do. If you don't think that anything that's been discussed—from cover design, to blurb writing, to ad development to administration, is worth your time or befitting to your skills set, take no shame in admitting it and move on to the next chapter, "Call in the Cavalry". If there are things that fit for you to take on, keep reading for tips and motivation.

THE BEAUTY **of DIY**

There are upsides to doing whichever of your marketing tasks that you can, yourself. Nobody knows your brand, or your books, as well as you. If you're like me, you don't want to spend all day in your characters' heads, even if you had the luxury. Regardless of what you write, taking care of your own marketing carries the following benefits:

- **Efficiency.** No going back and forth with someone you've hired on vision and execution; doing it yourself reduces the training burden and saves time spent getting on the same page
- **Transparency.** Instead of checking behind someone else's work or waiting for information about how an element of your marketing plan is coming along, you will maintain full visibility at all times.
- **Education.** Indeed, doing your own marketing makes you a stronger marketer. There's a case to be made that every author should try every area of marketing at some point. The best book marketers I know, even if they have transitioned to relying on professionals to do their marketing work, were waist-deep in their own marketing at some point.
- **Timeliness and Agility.** The less dependent you are on other people's lead times and deadlines, the more flexibility you have to pivot on new information and seamlessly react.
- **Less Clock-Watching = More Playing.** When

you hire someone at an agreed-upon price, it creates incentives for that person to stay in-scope. Sometimes, sticking only with what was contracted or what you hired somebody for compromises creativity and reduces the temptation to play with new ideas, experiment and test.

Yet, adding more to your own plate means committing extra time and taking on emotional stress. More marketing tasks to complete means more production deliverables and deadlines. It's doable through sheer grit and force of will, but it's even more doable with solid planning and the use of some smart tools.

- **Media Kits.** A media kit is a curated set of materials about each book you've released. You can also have a media kit about you as an author and your collected works as a whole. Media kits are modular. They centralize reusable content about each book that you might want to use over and over again: cover images, quotes and excerpts, ad copy, discount/sale language, the blurb, information about awards you've won, etc. Media kits save time because they collect the set of materials you will call upon repeatedly— preventing you from having to reinvent the wheel— throughout the course of marketing a single book.
- **Social Media Scheduling Tools.** Particularly if you're a full-time writer, with large chunks of your day to spend on your craft, posting and responding on social media can be interruptive. A scheduling tool, like HootSuite or Sprout Social, will make it easy to schedule your posts and streamline your ability to respond to what's coming through.
- **Courses.** Maybe you've committed to doing a lot of

this yourself, but you still require a lot of training. Find a reputable course that people you know can vouch for—but only after you've confirmed that the basic method aligns to your library. All of the vetting that you do of individual courses should come down to this. Find author friends with libraries, strengths and weaknesses similar to yours and ask candidly how well a specific course fit. Choosing the wrong course is a waste of time and money, and it may take you hours of hands-on work and weeks of trying a methodology that can't work for you before you realize your mistake.

IF YOU NEED **to Abandon Ship**

Not to be Debbie Downer, but it's possible, after deciding to fly solo, that you discover your plan just isn't working for your goals. Have you seen those shows on HGTV where ambitious homeowners decide to remodel their kitchen themselves? Then they have to call a contractor after they cause $10,000 in extra damage demolishing something that didn't need it or hitting a water main? Yeah. That happens with marketing.

If your abilities aren't measuring up, give it one more good try, but don't stick with it because you said you would or because you have something to prove. Your goal is to succeed in the way you've envisioned. There's no shame in hiring a professional if it's come to that. Marketing is a skilled profession. People go to school for it for a long time. Don't try to be a hero if you can't save the day.

14 CALL IN THE CAVALRY

IF YOU DON'T HAVE the skills, or just plain don't want to take on what's needed to get to your best plan, there can be great comfort in hiring the right professionals. Emphasis on *the right* professionals—not just someone who talks a good game. A phrase I've repeated to clients for many years whenever they've griped about previous marketing teams they've worked with is this: "Marketers are really good at marketing themselves."

I once read a statistic that said the average tenure that marketing agencies work with companies is fewer than two years. As a former agency marketer who pitched prospective clients, and sometimes lost business to agencies with weaker skills but a better dog-and-pony show, I saw firsthand how easy it was for people who didn't know much about marketing to be swayed by whoever seemed the smartest.

It's easy to be wooed by people who know more about any topic than you—people who seem polished and confident. Many authors have been burnt by marketers they hired who turned out to be the wrong talent. It's not that the marketers were necessarily bad, or that the authors were too naive. There are some snake oil salesmen out there, but most marketing relationships-gone-bad come down to misaligned expectations.

Here's what marketers know that lay people don't—something that responsible, transparent marketers will say directly to clients up front—something we understand down to the marrow of our bones: you fail for a long time before you succeed—such is the process of learning—and meaningful results take time.

The basic formula of marketing is simple: isolate what works the best, then see how well you can get the success formula to scale. Most marketing—especially early marketing, when a book is still getting its legs—is heavy on trial-and-error learning, which is just another way to say "failing". But I won't lie to you: the trial and error never ends. The marketplace changes constantly. Retailers change their algorithms; Costs-Per-Click (CPCs) fluctuate; category competition and other market dynamics shift.

If you're an author who has done digital marketing for a long time—who has run campaigns and done tracking, and who has an existing set of data to support what's working vs. what's not, the new marketer you hire has a shot at a running start. But especially if you aren't bringing much to the table in terms of knowing who is buying your books and engaging with your brand, you have to assume that your marketer needs space to do trial and error, and is starting at zero.

With all this in mind, the surest way to tell whether a marketer is overselling his capabilities is if said marketer seems ceaselessly optimistic about projected results. This is because you can do all the right things and still not make money at first. The marketing data itself shows what's working and not working and sometimes changes are required to get better results. Even a seasoned marketer who is very optimistic is wise not to make you any promises. Counterintuitive results happen all the time. A great marketer has the wisdom to under-promise and over-deliver.

Here is a list of what to be cautious of as you look to hire any marketer:

- **No direct experience in book marketing.** Just because you can market other products doesn't mean you can market books. I learned this one the hard way, myself. Even with all of my expertise and my sterling track record of ushering brands to success as an agency marketer, it took me two years of underperforming and, at times, failing completely before I figured out this book marketing thing. As it turned out, general marketing expertise wasn't enough, nor was my understanding of the industry as an author. I had to do research and learn from others before I even figured the ecosystem out. And, as I also realized, hiring marketers who are working with other authors (and who therefore bring current, relevant insights from their other authors) has value of its own.

- **Lack of professionalism.** I don't do all of my own marketing and believe me when I tell you, I interviewed hard. I pulled strings to gain access to some of the very best professionals. At one point, I was busy being impressed by a marketer who clearly knew his stuff. Frankly, I was ready to work with him —then he did a screen share with me and started showing me one of his other clients' numbers. I understood what he was doing, and why—he was showing me his results. He knew I'm a marketer, that I would understand what he was showing me, and that it would impress me. But if you get any inkling that the person you're speaking with won't be discreet or professional or on the up-and-up, run— don't walk. It's really not worth it to work with someone who might share your confidential data inappropriately with others.

- **Lack of a portfolio or references.** Any sort of professional should be ready to demonstrate that they are the expert they say they are and can get the results that they say they've gotten. Even without sharing client data, there's usually a way for marketers to show sanitized results or to tell you who their clients are and invite you to make a call for references. Always ask for references. Even if their qualifications seem clear. If they've left a trail of satisfied clients in their wake, those clients would be happy to speak with you.

- **Temptation to hire for the wrong reasons.** This is also a caution to authors tempted to tap their own networks to find someone who knows what they're doing. Just because your across-the-street neighbor's kid is a freelance marketer doesn't mean she's the write gal for the job. Same thing for your nephew who seems to understand social media better than you ever will. If you don't get this stuff at all, it's easy to lower your hiring bar to anyone who seems to know more than you. But your goal is to be successful at book marketing, and just because a marketer knows more than you doesn't mean he knows enough.

On the opposite end of hiring professionals who may not be qualified is a different sort of problem: authors who find amazing marketing talent but balk at the price. I've seen authors scoff at the idea of spending $300 a month on a marketer. But, folks...like I said a minute ago, marketing is a skilled profession. People who do it have college degrees or MBAs. Fair market value for a marketer who knows her stuff is $50-$150 per hour.

But let's say you're working with a marketer who thinks her time is only worth $25/hour. Anyone who's got a shot at moving the needle would have to spend 4-5 hours per week on your brand. Even at a below-market $25/hour, you're still in the $400-$500 a month range to have an expert spend the time needed to get better results for your brand.

A lot of authors I meet who "hired someone to do their marketing" paid said marketer a (low) price the author was comfortable with. The problem is, anyone who's charging that little needs a ton of clients to make ends meet and probably isn't working very hard for your brand.

Beyond that, any marketer worth her salt isn't going to take a third of what she's worth just so you can afford her. These misaligned economics are yet another reason why most authors who are getting real, expert marketing help are the authors with real budgets. Just like you don't like to be squeezed on your royalty payments, don't squeeze marketers on their fees. A good marketer will earn back her own value, and marketers need to earn a living wage, just like you.

15 YOU CAN DO THIS

THE END of this curriculum is always hard, especially when I deliver it to a live audience. This is a course that values realism over endless possibility. Let me be clear—you absolutely can achieve your goal, no matter how lofty it is. Know that you will get to it faster now that you are thinking through the reality of what that will actually take. And don't forget—businesses that succeed always require a tremendous amount of work and financial investment; they always make mistakes that must be learned, and from there, they learn how to recover; they gather experience, get smarter and persevere.

So, go back. Look at your plan. Review your goals and constraints. Cry a little if this will take a lot more time/money/effort than you thought. Grab some ice cream if you need to and a box of Kleenex. Talk through these concepts with your partner or spouse. Then, brush yourself off, look at your unique plan and be confident in what you can do. It's time to go forth and achieve.

WORDS OF THANKS

I always say that marketing is failing—having the bravery to do it over and over and the fortitude to stick with it until you learn enough to succeed. I wouldn't know half of what I know about book marketing if so many author-friends and clients hadn't been so candid about their own failures and so generous with their time, insights and tips.

Special thanks to Kara, Liz, Bex, Gail, and Caroline for keeping their ears to the ground, dropping kernels of wisdom and sharing what happened when they were bold. Thanks to Eva, Ro, and Melissa for being so great at what they do well that all I have to do, to learn from them, is watch. Thanks also to those who probably don't know how many great ideas I got from very brief conversations—Bobby and Nana come to mind. And I'm forever grateful for my larger communities where I meet wonderful people and hear great advice: I'm looking at you, San Francisco and Silicon Valley RWAs and SF Indie Uncon.

ABOUT KILBY BLADES

Kilby Blades is a 25-time-award-winning author of Romance and Women's Fiction. Critics laud her "feminist romance", noting heroes who wouldn't dream of inhibiting their women and heroines who wouldn't dream of letting them.

Her debut novel, *Snapdragon*, was a HOLT Medallion Award of Merit recipient, a Semi-Finalist in the Publisher's Weekly BookLife Prize, an IPPY Award medalist, and Kilby herself is the 2018 RSJ Emma Award honoree for Best Debut Author.

On the nonfiction side, Kilby is the author of *The Book Marketing Audit* and *Marketing Steamy Romance*. She has guest-written for Publisher's Weekly, Heroes and Heartbreakers, and is a regular contributor to the Romance Writers of America's *Romance Writer's Report*. She holds an MBA from the University of Chicago and is the originator of the *Six Figure Author* podcast and blog.

When she's not writing, Kilby goes to movie matinees alone, where she eats Chocolate Pocky and buttered popcorn and usually smuggles in not-a-little-bit of red wine. She procrastinates from the difficult process of writing by oversharing on Facebook and Instagram and giving away cool stuff to her newsletter subscribers. Kilby is a mother, a social-justice fighter, and above all else, a glutton for a good story.

facebook.com/kilbybladesauthor

twitter.com/kilbyblades

instagram.com/kilbyblades

bookbub.com/authors/kilby-blades

goodreads.com/kilbyblades

ALSO BY KILBY BLADES

Other Stories in the Hexagon Universe

Snapdragon

Chrysalis

Crazy Old Money: A BWWM Billionaire Romantic Comedy

Vertical: A BWWM Dark Romantic Comedy Novella

Young Adult and New Adult Rom-Com

The Art of Worship

Friended

The "Worst Day Ever" Anthology Series

Worst Holiday Ever: A Family Drama Romance Anthology

Worst Valentine's Day Ever: A Lonely Hearts Romance Anthology

Romantic Women's Fiction

The Secret Ingredient: A Curvy Girl Small Town Culinary Romance

Non-Fiction

Marketing Steamy Romance

Made in the USA
Middletown, DE
22 April 2019